EARLY PRAISE FOR
A LIFE INHERITED

"Captivating, moving, brilliant and like nothing you've ever read before. Lipiner-Katz writes her soul in this must-read book that will surely be cherished by so many."
—*Hen Mazzig, "The Algemeiner's"*
Top 100 People Positively Influencing Jewish Life, 2021

"Rena Lipiner Katz uses her masterful control of language to tell her spellbinding story of triumph over tragedy that is somehow unique to her position as the child of Holocaust survivors, and universal to anyone who has had to claw their way back from despair and heartbreak in order to find joy, success and, ultimately, peace."
—*Nancy Krulik, New York Times Best Selling Author.*

D1236100

A LIFE INHERITED

UNRAVELING THE TRAUMA OF A SECOND-GENERATION HOLOCAUST SURVIVOR

RENA LIPINER KATZ

WILBUR & DOLCE BOOKS

Wilbur & Dolce Books titles may be ordered from your favorite bookseller.

Visit
www.WilburandDolce.com

Wilbur & Dolce Books
c/o CMI Fulfillment
4822 South 133rd Street
Omaha, NE 68137

Hardcover: 979-8-9870916-1-6
Paperback: 979-8-9870916-2-3
Kindle: 979-8-9870916-3-0
Audiobook: 979-8-9870916-4-7
Library of Congress Control Number: 2022918737

Author Photo: Mayan Toledano
Publishing Services provided by: Concierge Publishing Services

Printed in the United States of America

10 9 8 7 6 5 4 3 2 1

CONTENTS

INTRODUCTION

This is a true story; however, I have changed the names of some individuals to protect the privacy of my children. Even as adults, they are innocents and the ultimate victims.

PART I

CHAPTER 1

THE FIRST TIME
(1991)

I was pregnant the first time it happened. Saying "it happened" rather than "he did this to me" allows it to remain at a safe distance, even now decades later, and the language I use foretells my story as I lift responsibility away from my husband.

We had been married nearly a year and were living in the apartment I had rented since graduate school. The building, constructed in the 1920s, was on Manhattan's Upper West Side, and the apartment had two airy bedrooms, high ceilings, and honey-colored oak floors arranged in a herringbone pattern. Light came in from the west over the Hudson River.

It was late spring and I was four months pregnant with Noah, my first. I recall two things vividly: the sun spilling in through the open windows of the bedroom, and what I wore that day—a navy cotton maternity dress, a delightful hand-me-down from the wife of one of Brian's softball buddies. Whenever I wore it, I remembered the blue sailor dress I had loved as a child. Light and loose, the dress accommodated my growing belly and had two rows of gold buttons down the front. The rest I see as if I were watching myself in a film.

I believed that I had caused Brian to lose control, provoking him by contradicting something he said. What was unusual this time was that I would not take back my offending words. Feeling stronger than I had in a while, probably because of the baby, I stood my ground and told Brian to leave. I could not be married to him anymore, I said. In fat bundles, I lifted his shirts and jackets from the closet and threw them into his gray duffel bag that lay on the floor.

The hangers scattered and, picking one up, Brian began to hit me with it. I was not surprised, for I had seen this possibility in his eyes before. I was relieved it had finally emerged; I needed to see my monster. Instinctively I turned my body so that I faced away from him. Arms crisscrossed over my front, I fell onto the bed holding my stomach and the blows landed on my back.

After a few minutes, Brian became winded and walked out of the bedroom. It was quiet again, and I could hear the cars on the street below. I don't remember feeling much of anything, but when I pulled myself up, I noticed the afternoon sun streaming in past the purple-and-white flowered curtains my mother had sewn when I had first moved in. It was then that I became frightened that we might have been seen by people who lived in the buildings across the street. What would they think?

How mangled my thinking was then, but in retrospect and with compassion I could not make my way through the feelings that squared off inside me. Feelings that reduced to ash what I knew to be right. The horror I felt that the man I had married could hurt our baby was rationalized away by my belief that I had caused his eruption. And if it were my fault, I could prevent it from happening again. I know this now, but the feelings did not make their way to consciousness then.

Ten years later, when I told my love my secrets, he wore his poker face. Though he tried to force his features to contain what he felt, I saw grief in the crease between his eyes and the twitch in his jaw. From the moment we had come together, Ron had been driven to protect me.

"But he hit me on the back," I told him, "not on the belly."

"You really believe there's a difference? Do you understand what you are saying? What you are *thinking*—that there was some part of his violence that was okay, even justifiable?"

"Yes, there *is* a difference," I said. "He didn't want to hurt the baby."

I understood rationally that I was talking nonsense, but what I had always felt floating inside of me, so easily ignited by any failing or misstep, was the pervasive sense that I was defective and deserved to be hurt. I was certain that Brian had not hurt the wife before me, or the two that came afterward. I believed these women would not stand for it, that they were made of different stuff. That there was something about me that *demanded* to be hurt. My heart breaks now for the woman I was.

Yet how much of who I was had grown from a need to come closer to what my parents had endured during the Holocaust, to be scapegoated and victimized? It is impossible to quantify. Psychology theorists might suggest that I needed to master my parents' experience as survivors by creating and reliving a kind of facsimile of their early lives—the physical uncertainty, the constant sensation of helplessness, and the brutalization. Had I been primed to find my own Nazi?

CHAPTER 2

THE END OF CHILDHOOD
(1940)

Through the train's window, the glass clouded with the prints of small fingers, a dark-haired, blue-eyed child of seven squints as she watches her mother walk away from the tracks into the adjacent woods. The woman does not look back as her daughter silently implores her to. It is July 1940, and the Soviet train traveling from eastern Poland to Siberia has just eased into the station. The child's mother has stepped off the rancid cattle car, stuffed now with human beings, to find food for her children. Lusia tracks her mother as she is swallowed up by the thicket, one limb after another fading until she is gone.

The train stops for half an hour or more, its massive metal doors clanking fearsomely as they slide open to allow the passengers to relieve themselves. Lusia is terrified the train will leave before her mother, Rose, returns from what is usually a fool's errand. Even so, Rose leaves the train each time the engines sputter and die.

Lusia, who would become my mother a decade and a half later in another part of the world, is a child who believes her steadfast gaze will keep her family whole. She tries to shepherd her parents and older sister—though they are too absorbed in their own preoccupations to notice—insisting that they sit in one corner of the train, close to the doors. She does not want them to be wedged in by the crowd, should they need to get out quickly. Lusia shivers, her heart banging in the bony envelope of her chest as her breaths come hard but shallow. Stress hormones flood her brain, sending directives to terminals in her body. She feels as if she is drowning.

Since the war began, Lusia had watched her parents, Abe and Rose, lose what was so recognizable about them: an ease with life and the world they inhabited. Now their world had become fraught with danger at every turn, and her parents had become obsessively protective, refusing to allow their daughters to be out on their own, insisting that they walk together or as part of a group.

Before the war began in September 1939, before the family had run from the Nazi army that would occupy their town, Sucha, and hunt its Jews, Lusia had freedom to roam. She picked flowers and blueberries by the river, bought hot rolls at the bakery, and at the open-air market she would skip from vendor to vendor receiving candy and smiles. Now Lusia's parents had stopped smiling and did not tease or play with her anymore. Abe was no longer jaunty and rakishly handsome but grim and tightly wound. Rose was depressed—she missed the loving camaraderie she had known with her sisters and brothers. Their faces were like masks with eyes always on alert, always looking. Everything about them seemed to pull downward as if their bodies (so light and airy before) had been overcome by gravity. They were thin, and the clothes they wore, once filled out by flesh, hung from their frames. Despite being lighter in weight, they walked more heavily now, sinking into the ground with steps that fell like lead. Their nonchalant elegance was gone.

As tension spilled over everything, Abe and Rose fought with each other now, sometimes about Lusia and her sister, Frieda. Once, Lusia heard her mother cry and beg Abe to return home to Poland, back to the family they'd left behind. What shocked Lusia more than her mother's tears was the anger and determination in her father's response.

"Go back if you must to the Nazis. But you will not take the girls!"

I believe it was during the ten years of their displacement, from 1939 to 1949, that my mother's experiences and her own parents' behavior determined how she would eventually raise me and my younger brother.

As Lusia watched her mother grow more fearful, a template of motherhood began to be etched in her mind. Rose agonized about uprooting her daughters from the only home they had ever known, but most distressing for her was the unrelenting scarcity of food. How could Lusia make sense of her mother pushing her own bread rations into her daughters' hands, claiming she was not hungry? Hunger was a constant now, and the conflict tore at Lusia's heart.

Whenever my mother told me this story—I cannot remember a time when the stories were new, when I had not known everything, when the life my parents had lived was not *my* everything—her eyes would flood instantly. She was help-less to control tears that came from the place that had only ever held her mother.

"How could I possibly take my mother's piece of bread if I thought she was hungry?" she asked me, her eyes widening at my obtuseness. "I had to believe her!"

I will never know how my mother might have diverged from the person she was had she not lived the Holocaust. But during the moments that she tracked my grandmother's movements away from the cattle car, and in the millions of moments of war that followed, the emotional apparatus that my mother would need to endure the war, and later mother her own children, would form and reform.

From a high-spirited, trusting child, Lusia morphed into someone whose only purpose was to hold everything close lest she lose what mattered most. Whether it was a barrette that kept her hair from her eyes, the rags that covered her feet when she outgrew her one pair of shoes, or her precious family, Lusia transformed into an eagle-eyed child-adult. Much like her father, she became someone who took on the task of keeping track of everyone and everything.

And because of the experiences that shocked my mother's system, certain changes may have occurred deep in her cells, far below what could be seen. The theory of epigenetics holds that the way one's DNA—the genotype—*behaves* may be altered when children are exposed to extreme trauma. The genes themselves are not changed, but the phenotype—*how* genes are expressed, manifesting in what is observable in an individual, like brown eyes or a predisposition to experience certain emotions—is remodeled.

According to the Centers for Disease Control, "Epigenetics is the study of how your behaviors and environment can cause changes that affect the way your genes work. Unlike genetic changes, epigenetic changes are reversible and do not change your DNA sequence, but they can change how your body reads a DNA sequence."[1]

With the advent of improved diagnostic tools, research has shown that children of Holocaust survivors may have more intense stress responses than are found in the general population.

"The Holocaust left its visible and invisible marks not only on the survivors, but also on their children," said Dr. Natan

Kellerman. "Instead of numbers tattooed on their forearms, however, they may have been marked epigenetically with a chemical coating upon their chromosomes, which would represent a kind of biological memory of what the parents experienced. As a result, some suffer from a general vulnerability to stress while others are more resilient."

He explained, "Previous research assumed that such transmission was caused by environmental factors, such as the parents' childbearing behavior. New research, however, indicates that these transgenerational effects may have been also (epi)genetically transmitted to their children. Integrating both hereditary and environmental factors, epigenetics adds a new and more comprehensive psychobiological dimension to the explanation of transgenerational transmission of trauma."[2]

What my mother saw and experienced during the war, the environment in which she grew, and the physiological ways her body's cells and her mind reacted to that environment shaped how she would forever move through the world. And it was the interplay of these elements throughout my mother's childhood that influenced the person and mother I would become. Whether it was caused by epigenetics or nurture, or a chemistry of both that laid most of the foundation, I cannot know.

By the time she became my mother, Lusia had evolved into a loving, anxious woman, a relentless fighter, a protector who knew that the world had the potential to decimate the ones she loved. The terror of this awareness rooted inside her, and later in me.

In the broadest of strokes, my father's experience of the Holocaust was much like my mother's. Yet somehow he emerged from the war with his innate optimism and capacity to feel joy still intact. My father was like sunshine. Through the medium of his continuous loving attention, I absorbed his miraculous capacity to embrace a world that could so quickly become pernicious. But the fruit of this ability was spoiled by my ever-present guilt for having been gifted life through my parents' survival.

As I internalized the *ways* in which my parents responded to the Holocaust, their physiological and emotional memories of events transformed into mine, informing my feelings, thoughts, and behaviors for years. The way I mothered my own children, the fences real and imagined I built around them, the thousands of choices I made along the way all had their origins in events that predated my existence by a decade—events that bequeathed to me living memories of the inferno that was the Holocaust.

When the story of my family in Europe first became the genesis of mine, when the number *six million* took on impossible meaning, I could almost feel the horror of being hunted and praying for deliverance. Until I was twelve, I needed my parents to check each door and window at night, then tuck me into bed before I could fall asleep. But even after this ritual, my mind was stuffed with grotesque creatures in shadow. I did not believe that my parents were omniscient like many young children do; I knew there were no parents who could win a fight against the Nazis, and survive. The only thing that could be done was to hide.

My thoughts and fantasies flitted between outrunning the Nazis, escaping Auschwitz where my grandmother's family had been killed, and bringing their murderers to judgement. Later, when I was an adult and new mother, visions of the Nazi practice of killing a child in full view of the mother would fly unbidden through my mind, leaving me wrecked in their wake.

This was the string that pulled at me throughout my life. It coiled and knotted dread around my core, and fear was what I became most familiar with. Marked by battles I had not experienced, fearfulness was the backbone of my emotional core, and guilt lay just beneath the fear. Guilt for having been born because my mother and father had survived. These emotions led me to certain ways of being in the world, and the paths I took were often predetermined. Spontaneous choices were almost impossible because specific criteria had to be met: to delay or forgo pleasure, to suffer.

Throughout my childhood and into adulthood I often felt anxiety if wore pretty clothes; I worried that something terrible would happen to me or my family because of my vanity. I remember a mint-green silk blouse whose satin touch I adored, sitting unworn in a drawer. If I was not on guard, I would get knocked to the ground.

Pleasure was found in helping, or even better, saving, and I was usually compelled to intervene when I saw a person or an animal being hurt. I brought home stray cats and kittens. Once I gathered up a pigeon with a broken wing, delivered him to a vet, and paid for treatment when even the vet advised me not to. When he told me that the pigeon would never fly again, the panic I felt was like the grip of a steel claw. Perverse as it was, I felt I did not deserve to live in peace or know joy, and grief was my unconscious driver.

I first began to consider a different side of my parents' story, a narrative that did not revolve around them purely as victims, when I became a mother. I understood that it was not only a matter of good fortune that my parents had lived: it was their own parents' resilience in the face of a hellish, constantly changing environment. Years later it became a blueprint for my own survival, and I remained unaware of it even as it was being ingrained into me. Throughout the war, my grandparents had been reduced to beings who existed to protect their children, and they prevailed. To survive in a world that has been turned on its head requires one to change and adapt; that is how they survived the war.

After a decades-long process of integrating experiences that had never been mine to own, I came to realize that by living a life of self-oppression, rejecting the concept of fighting back, instead clutching only guilt and fear, I was, in effect, acting as a proxy for the Nazis. And that was the antithesis of honoring those who had been murdered. Rather, I could be free to flourish, even triumph. I could love, I could laugh, and I could change my mindset. This insight was not a sudden epiphany. It had come from moving through the stages and relationships in my life, motherhood, two marriages as different as could be, and seeing myself as not having simply emerged from a place of inevitable reactivity and vulnerability, but as someone who was raised with an endowment that had to be dismantled to be understood.

At birth, I was bequeathed the legacy of the Holocaust, by the very fact of my parents' survival. Starting out raw and hurting, I had to challenge that labyrinth of pain, to feel it and to mourn, but learn to live without its yoke. Working through this endowment was, for me, an incremental process. And though the impact of the Holocaust became no less weighty on my soul, it no longer determined how I charted the course of my life.

CHAPTER 3

CHILD OF WAR
(SEPTEMBER 1939)

My mother was six and finally starting school. She has told me the story of her school uniform more than once... more than a few times. It was the uniform she never wore. It was made to order just for her and hung on the door of the armoire so Lusia could see and touch it, anticipating the approaching day when she would first wear it. Summer was nearly over; sweet-scented afternoons spent picking blueberries and tagging along with her big sister to the river had ended and the evening air had cooled.

Their two-story house in the scenic Polish valley town of Sucha Beskidzka was made of brick and stone and had been in her father's family for generations. It sat on the edge of the town's square: a coveted site, my mother would say with pride. "I could look out of my window and see the *whole* town square! Market days were my favorite. Mama would send me to the bakery across the square to buy fresh rolls—they were still hot—and she'd give me five 'groshen' to spend on anything I wanted. I was in heaven!"

The family lived on the upper two floors; on the ground level my grandfather Abe presided over a general store. My mother was a self-professed naughty child referred to as "Marshall" by neighbors who heard her howls when she was displeased. Lusia bided no one except her father, who found her amusing no matter what mischief she was into. He would look the other way when, with great pleasure, she would dip her arms and hands deep into the massive barrels of grain in the store, the feel of it a delight on her skin.

Throughout the summer, the adults had grown restless, and my mother was anxious to know why. In the evenings, the aunts and uncles gathered at their house and spoke agitatedly while listening to a man's frenetic voice shouting on the radio, a man they referred to as "Hitler." It was clear the grown-ups were troubled and did not notice my mother crouched under the table, listening.

By then the news was everywhere: war was imminent. The aggressions of Germany continued unopposed, and no one knew if Britain or the United States would have the stomach or the military might to stop Hitler's land and power grab. When the Soviet Union and Germany signed a nonaggression pact in August 1939, my grandfather Abe believed that Poland would soon be divided up by Germany and the Soviet Union.

Abe had spent weeks maneuvering pins around a map trying to convince his siblings to travel east toward the Soviet Union. It was well known that, unlike the Nazis, the Russians had no appetite for killing Jews. My mother remembers an emotional discussion at the end of August, her father deeply upset; his hands shook and his voice was thunder through the room.

"We cannot stay here, hiding! Everyone knows we are Jews. Why should we wait like lambs to be slaughtered?"

"Abe, calm down, you are not thinking clearly—you are being too emotional. We don't know what the Germans will do when they arrive here," said his brother, Mehul, older by ten years, who had protected Abe after the early death of their father. "Nobody is chasing us from our homes."

My grandfather had been pacing, and he stopped short. "Yes, we *do* know what will happen, Mehul. Just look at what is going on in Germany. It's not enough for those bastards that Jews—patriotic Germans—were completely stripped of their rights, their citizenship. Jews are considered vermin—they are being *shot* in the streets."

"But Abe, how can we possibly travel such a distance, with winter coming?" his brother asked. "And where do we go? We will run straight into the German army or the Soviets."

"Not if we plan our route carefully. We go strictly east and take only the smallest dirt roads—the German army will have to use the main roads."

His audience was listening now, their resistance eroding by the force of Abe's will. The emotional temperature of the room was lowering.

"We have no choice—they will be here in days, a week at the most. And while I am still breathing, I will never look at a Nazi uniform."

Bronia, Abe's youngest sister, agreed. "Abe is right, we have to get out of Sucha—it's too dangerous to stay put. We can get to the eastern frontier. The Russians don't hate Jews—they even have Jewish soldiers. Once we are there, they will not hurt us."

My mother told me that my grandmother Rose said little but her face was an open book. Rose was miserable at the prospect of leaving. Her sisters and brothers meant everything to her, and, citing responsibilities, had already announced they would not leave their homes. Abe finally prevailed and fourteen members of his family agreed to his plan, leaving nearly every aspect of their lives behind.

I often wondered how I would have behaved under the same circumstances. The answer is simple. Because the Holocaust was my scorched birthright—its verdict—I would have taken my children and fled sooner than they had. But in 1939 there was no benefit of hindsight, and without it I am not sure I would have left everything that I had built in my life. Most Polish Jews, like Abe's brother, Mehul, and Rose's siblings, believed that the German army would come, they would stay for a while, and after some borders were moved, they would leave. Life would return to normal, just as it had so many times before in that part of Eastern Europe where borders were pushed and pulled and manipulated every couple of decades.

It was September first, Friday night, the first Sabbath of the month, and my mother and Frieda were awoken by my grandmother some hours before dawn. Rose was subdued, and the girls clamored for an explanation.

"Mama, Mama, what is going on, why do we have to wake up now?"

"It's still dark, Mama," Frieda murmured, half asleep.

My grandmother cast her eyes around the room and spoke in a rushed tone. "Papa has decided we are going to take a short vacation to visit your cousins. You both need to get up now and hurry. I want you to dress and put on as many layers as you can. Wear two dresses, a sweater, a pair of slacks, and a coat. Now hurry!"

It was barely fall, and my mother and Frieda, who was then eight, were confused by their mother's instructions. But that was all the information they were given, and my mother remembers how reluctant and distracted my grandmother Rose was, how speaking seemed difficult for her. My mother believes to this day that Rose, so ambivalent about leaving her sisters and brothers behind, would have stayed if not for Abe's insistence.

Aunts and uncles and cousins—ten in all—were waiting outside the house, the children already seated on top of a wagon pulled by a skinny horse. The driver stood waiting, silent. My mother watched as Rose began to panic. Her voice high, Rose called out to my grandfather, "Abe! Where are the keys? We have to lock the door—the silver is still inside."

My grandfather laughed, "Rose! Do you think a lock will keep the Germans out?"

And then my mother knew that she would not be starting school. The children and pregnant cousin Bella rode on top of the wagon where bundles were loaded. The rest of the adults walked and bickered about where they should ultimately land, but they all agreed that it would be disastrous if Bella were to give birth on the road. A baby would make everyone more vulnerable.

As my grandfather was the acknowledged leader of the group, the family felt free to blame him whenever they believed a bad decision had been made. He took the brunt of their fear, their anger, and periodically, during the next six years, the responsibility for the conditions they would find themselves in.

The stories I heard about my grandfather recalled the biblical zealots I had learned about from the young Hasidic scholar who taught my childhood Hebrew school class. Abe's decision to leave came from a place of hurt and distrust—the orphaned remains of an impoverished childhood observing and experiencing the anti-Semitism of his Polish neighbors. He could have been viewed as a paranoid outlier, but his suspicions of possible betrayal by his neighbors would be borne out.

My mother told me that a Pole could receive half a kilo of sugar for turning in a Jew. A family of six could net three kilos. Yet far more often, she spoke about the "Righteous Gentiles," the people who hid Jews at the risk of brutal Nazi punishment. I often thought about this: whether I would shelter someone at the risk of my own children's safety. Would I protect them, feed them, care for their physical needs for the duration of that war? I think that my own brand of selfishness would not let me bear the guilt I would feel if I refused to save a life. And my imaginings were still so far from the horrific reality of the situation.

Abe had felt the cataclysm coming from the west. In his youth, he had seen frothing mobs turn into bloody pogroms and at sixteen had been attacked and nearly beaten to death by three men. They kicked and pummeled him, shrieking, "Kill the Jew, kill the Jew!" Wrestled to the ground by the ringleader, Abe pulled his enormous iron ring of keys from his pocket and slammed it into the man's head. The two other men were shocked and frozen in place as my grandfather ran off.

Abe had been closely following the news out of Germany: the rise of Adolph Hitler and the German Reich and the 1935 Nuremberg Race Laws. These laws declared Jews an inferior race and revoked their German citizenship. Jews were now barred from professions, universities, and neighborhoods. As Hitler eyed Polish land, Abe knew that with its weak and poorly equipped military, Poland was ripe for the taking. Austria had already been annexed by Germany, and part of Czechoslovakia had been invaded. In 1939 when Stalin and Hitler formed their nonaggression pact, it was understood that Poland would soon be carved up between the two powers, with the Soviet Union taking eastern Poland. Abe knew they would not survive occupation by the German army.

My grandfather was farsighted, and the crucial elements along his mental roadmap were precisely calculated. The amount of money that would be required for the months-long journey, resources needed for the children, when the horse would rest and feed, and what to do if Bella went into labor.

Always anticipating the next hurdle, Abe had to know that everyone under his stewardship was, and would be, safe.

Once, when my grandfather was ill from typhus, he was incoherent as he pointed repeatedly to the interior wall of their room. Afterward, when he had recovered, he explained that what he had tried but failed to show his wife and daughters was a spot between two stones where he had lodged a thick gold coin.

"This," he said, "is for our lives. Not for bread, not for anything else, just for our lives." They knew this meant it was to be used as a payoff to escape, or for lifesaving medicine.

The family caravan of fourteen traveled for nearly three months amid heavy rains and Nazi bombs. At the beginning of the journey, the countryside was strewn with the dead. Once, as German bombs screamed to the earth, my grandfather threw himself on top of his daughters, completely covering their bodies so that his was the only form visible from the sky.

When the planes had finished their work and flown away, my mother saw an old woman and her horse lying still as fallen statues at the edge of a crater that a Luftwaffe bomb had blown into the earth. She said the woman's kerchief was still tied neatly under her chin. At first, struggling to process the sight, Lusia thought that the woman and her horse were sleeping. But she felt that this sleep was different.

"It seemed like the end of a chapter, the end of everything," she told me. Witnessing this carnage for the first time, my mother felt something inside her shift, a fundamental change that she was unprepared for. The understanding shattered previous beliefs—that God watched over everything, that her mother and father would always protect her. Sitting on top of the wagon, from that point forward she insisted one of her parents hold her hand always.

After three months on the road, they arrived at the Russian zone in eastern Poland, now part of the Soviet Union. There, my grandparents separated from the extended family and with their girls found shelter in a tiny hunter's hut in the forest until June 1940.

One night Russian soldiers banged at their door. The soldiers barked at them as the family roused quickly. "Get up, collect your things, you are leaving here!"

My mother remembers her father shrinking before her eyes as he submissively asked where they were being taken. She pulled and tugged at his arms and his pant leg trying to free her fierce father from the skin of this new meek man.

"Don't ask questions, just move!" barked the soldier who appeared to be in charge. My mother began to cry. When I first heard this story, I asked why she cried.

"I cried for the loss of my father as I knew him," she said. But Abe reclaimed his authority when they met the extended family at the train station. My mother understood that in the presence of the soldiers he had adopted a demeanor of someone unthreatening who could be safely ignored.

Given only half an hour to gather their belongings, the family had walked with the soldiers to the now-teeming train station. Everyone there was to be deported to a labor camp in Siberia where their constant companions would be hunger, disease, cold, and lice. Yet my mother always reminded me of what was most important.

"We were always *together*," she would say. And I learned quickly that the glue of life was family.

A year later, in June 1941, Hitler was unsatisfied with the lands he had already conquered and invaded the Soviet Union. Hitler's invasion was called Operation Barbarossa, and he hoped to continue east to conquer Moscow. The Jews who still lived in the town my mother's family had been deported from were massacred by the "Einsatzgruppen" (deployment groups), an army of death squads whose purpose was to murder Jews and those who were anti-Nazi, clearing the way for the regular German army.

This deportation to Siberia saved my family. The Soviets stopped the German army in the Battle of Moscow, and because of Hitler's invasion, the Soviets joined the Allied forces, a crucial step toward the eventual Allied victory.

Soon afterward, Jews and other refugees who had been sent to Siberia were granted permission to leave for different parts of the Soviet Union, areas with more hospitable weather. My grandfather once again gathered the extended family and announced that they would now travel south to Central Asia where there were Jewish communities and a more temperate climate.

In August 1941, the family started their six-week journey, again by cattle car, to Tajikistan. There they stayed, living in shacks built in the courtyards of the homes of Bukharan Jewish families. Fed and sheltered by the families who had been urged by their community's rabbi to "adopt" Jewish refugees, they lived in Tajikistan for five more years until the end of the war.

In 1946, Joseph Stalin finally allowed refugees to leave the Soviet Union. And it was only then as my mother and her family traveled west toward Poland that they began to hear rumors of horrific events, of massacres and then of the concentration camps. My grandmother Rose refused to believe the stories she heard. She put up notices wherever she could, asking if anyone had seen her sisters, Chava and Chana, or her brothers, Isaac and David. She would tell her daughters, "Don't worry, we will find them. You will see, they are alive—they are looking for us too."

But my grandmother's family had not believed Abe's predictions of a Nazi death machine. They thought he was hysterical, paranoid, and not a student of history. After all, they said, Jews had been always targeted; this was not new. How could they pick up and leave their homes and their businesses? It was simply not possible.

When my mother finally arrived in Poland with her parents and sister, they rested in Krakow on their way—finally!—back to Sucha. My grandfather managed to find an old school friend who was not Jewish. His friend was distraught and implored my grandfather not to return.

"Avrum," he said, "please don't come back. They are killing Jews so they can steal their houses. You will not be safe—*they will murder you!*"

My mother recalls hostile stares when they walked on the streets of Krakow. One time, she heard people laugh and say, "Look! They are back. The un-slaughtered chickens have come back!"

And then my grandmother Rose learned that after being deported from the ghetto the Nazis had forced them into, her four sisters and brothers and her nieces and nephews had been murdered in the gas chambers in Auschwitz in 1942. Murdered holding their babies and small children—all with peach skin and tiny hands and fingers that held on tight. Abe's beloved older brother Mehul, who had been like a father to him, was killed by an angry neighbor, and Mehul's wife and children were deported to Auschwitz where they were murdered..

It is in this context that I can best understand how my father and his family maintained their ability to embrace life after the war. He and his younger brother and parents had been spared the most soul-wrenching punishment the war would inflict: the loss of immediate family members. My father's father, Edmund, had two brothers. One lived in Philadelphia, and the other—a young Zionist—lived in Mandatory Palestine. My father's mother, Regina, had two younger brothers who had traveled with her and her family throughout the war.

My mother often said that what should have been the happiest days of their lives, being reunited with the loved ones who stayed behind, turned into the most hideous of nightmares. It was then that my grandfather made the decision to leave Poland without returning to Sucha. Abe told his family, "We will not go back there. All of Europe is soaked in Jewish blood."

They traveled west with others who had survived. The survivors had emerged from the woods, from the death marches, from Auschwitz and Chelmo and Majdanek, broken and tortured beyond comprehension. And there were those who had cheated the gas chambers and crematoria as the Nazis frantically tried to eliminate the evidence of genocide by murdering as many souls as possible before the imminent arrival of the Allied troops. They were the lost, the starved, the bereft and orphaned—a trail of humanity. They traversed a bombed-out European landscape that had been emptied of six million of their own.

At the age of fifteen, my mother went with her family to a displaced persons camp in Germany where they awaited permission to enter the United States. In 1949, America had taken in my family when its immigration quota was raised to give refuge to hundreds of thousands of stateless refugees. My mother watched her parents weep as their ship sailed into New York Harbor, passing the Statue of Liberty. "We were truly the 'tired and the poor,'" she said, referring to Emma Lazarus's poem inscribed at the base of the statue.

CHAPTER 4

LUSIA AND EDWARD
(1949)

The train traveled north through Germany carrying Polish refugees to the rusted cargo ship that would take them to America. My mother, Lusia, sat apart from her sister and her parents longing for relief from the darkness that enveloped them and caused them to appear folded into themselves.

The shock of comprehending the incomprehensible had undone her mother and father, and for a while they ceased to parent their teenage daughters. Between them they had lost twenty sisters, brothers, nieces, and nephews. The end of the war had released my mother's parents in name only, with each continuing to exist in the spaces carved out by those years.

My father, Edward, was also on that train. Blond, tall, and angular, with lime green eyes that saw Lusia completely, he pulled the sixteen-year-old girl away from the darkness with a brilliant smile and outstretched hands holding a tin coffee pot.

"Would you like some coffee?" He said this in Polish, confident in the veracity of his deduction based on her appearance and that of the small family sitting on the other side of the train's aisle watching him closely. And my mother's internal wings, which had lain flat and heavy throughout the war, rose to meet him because they were already a pair. They spoke for hours, the coffee pot set away.

My mother said she felt blinded by him, as though he were an apparition in the sun, and she would have done anything to keep him and his smile near, despite the glare coming from her father's eyes. "I had not seen anyone smile like that in years!"

On the boat to America, Edward—proficient in English, Russian, German, and Polish—was given the job of assigning work to the able-bodied passengers. To my grandfather Abe he gave the task of painting the ship's chimney so Edward would be free to romance my mother, far from Abe's heavy-browed scowl. But after docking in New York, Edward and Lusia lost each other amid the grasping reunions of the boat's passengers. My mother pined for him until one evening he appeared at her door. She was overjoyed that he had found her and hid his shoes in a far closet so the evening could be lengthened by an extra hour or so.

Although my mother dutifully registered for high school, her first day was her last. She would say, exhaling wistfully, "You know, I just didn't fit in. The girls were so pretty; they were wearing red lipstick and tight sweaters. Everyone and *everything* was so strange to me. Besides, I needed to make money to help Mama and Papa."

Edward took charge of the situation and found her a job at Orbach's department store where he worked. It was in midtown near its celebrated big sister, Macy's, and my mother was assigned to a back stockroom where the new hires with heavy accents were placed.

On the weekends my parents would take in a movie at Times Square or stroll through Central Park, mesmerized by the tall buildings on its perimeter, elixirs for eyes and minds that still worked to banish the grim images of war that had been imprinted. Sometimes they would have dinner at Horn & Hardart Automat where the little glass doors lifted miraculously to offer dazzling dishes for twenty-five cents.

Soon, Edward grew tired of the long subway and bus ride from Greenpoint to my mother's apartment in Bensonhurst, and he found a new place closer to his own for Lusia and her family. It was larger and less expensive than their first apartment, which had an unused room the sullen landlord locked with a heavy padlock so it could not be used.

Two years later they married, and Lusia—her name now a more culturally appropriate Lucy—wore her sister's wedding dress. In the photos, my mother beamed, but her sister's face had already lost its luminescence since her own wedding the year before. My mother's honeymoon trousseau—consisting of a halter dress, a red-and-white checked blouse, shorts, and a bathing suit, all from Orbach's—was forgotten on the subway ride home. She laughed at me when I told her she must have left them behind out of guilt for marrying—for living. The honeymoon pictures showed a jubilant pair, long-legged and stunning, with a backdrop of palm trees on the Miami trip. I was born three years later.

My mother was tightly bound to her parents and her sister. They had survived the war by thinking of themselves as one moving system rather than four individuals. Growing up, I remember my mother spending many weekends with her sister, Aunt Frieda, and their parents after Frieda ran away from her husband, taking her little boy with her. She moved to an apartment in the building where my grandparents lived.

Frieda was gentle, softer than my mother, and had married a pious man who received her parents' approval because he was an Orthodox Jew who prayed three times a day and had a clothing shop in the South Bronx. Frieda did not want to marry him. Only twenty, she believed she had time, but he pursued her hard. She was sweet and vibrant, her dark beauty evocative of Ivanhoe's Rachel.

One day, after a nasty battle with her father about the approaching wedding, she kicked through a glass pane in the French door that separated the living room from the bedroom in their apartment. The glass shattered and her blood dripped on the spotless floor. After that, everything was quiet and she married. Soon she had a baby girl. A few years later, this child was followed by Barry, a gorgeous, blond, blued-eyed boy, plump and smiling. Frieda adored Barry. We were all in love with him—his jubilation at being alive.

I was nearly four when Barry died in his crib. I had been napping curled up with my father on the sofa, but I can still see the scene like a scratched film playing in front of my eyes. Frieda and Lusia had gone on a rare afternoon outing to see a movie—two pretty young women out and about, free for the afternoon.

I was awakened to light footfalls up the stairs that separated our two apartments and a high voice calling out that Barry had died. I knew loosely that death meant goodbye, but the permanence of it was not something I had considered. It was an inconceivable reach then. I neither saw nor heard what happened when the sisters returned home. I imagine my father took me away somewhere. But how would he have left my mother to face the agony of it alone, to see her sister's lifeblood drain away?

I tortured myself periodically with the thought of Barry leaving the world alone without his mother's touch, looking for her. Years later, they told me it was Sudden Infant Death Syndrome that took him.

"But wasn't he too old for that?" I asked.

Another thought was that Barry had suffered an allergic reaction to the vaccination he had received the day before. Why couldn't they make up their minds? The explanations seemed haphazard and ate away at me. When I think of him and the day he died, my body needs to propel itself somewhere, anywhere, but I am paralyzed, hemorrhaging with grief because I don't know what happened to him and I cannot change it. If one child gone is such an agony, how can the mind absorb one and a half million children murdered in the Holocaust? It is not possible. Maybe this is how human beings protect themselves from madness.

Frieda did not go to the funeral; her hands could not be pried from the rails of the crib. She lay underneath it on the floor for three days. Her future was sealed now. Her life was all but over, all that was left to do was breathe for sixty more years. Eleven months later, another son was born, and she loved him very much. Frieda never spoke of Barry again.

CHAPTER 5

THE MAN WHO TRIED TO ERASE
THE JEWS (1961)

My childhood was a mixed bag of utterly joyful, luminous moments and ones of pure terror and hopelessness. Everything in my family always, in one way or another, seemed to relate back to the Holocaust.

When I was six, the architect of Jewish extermination, Adolph Eichmann, was hunted down in Argentina and brought to Israel disguised as a hungover El Al pilot. My mother and father celebrated his capture by the Mossad, Israel's national intelligence agency, with an intensity I had never seen in them before. Joyous energy flowed all around as they danced, filling the spaces of our home and falling like phosphorescence.

The televising of Eichmann's trial was a first—an international broadcast. Along with *Romper Room* and *Captain Kangaroo*, the courtroom of the trial was one of my first memories of the television that sat on a wooden chest in my parents' bedroom. The room had not yet been configured as such because we had only just moved from the tiny apartment in the concrete flatlands of central Queens, where the principal view was an endless gray rolling cemetery. Our new home was a red

brick Cape at the far end of New York City, within spitting distance of the greener and more expensive grass of Long Island.

My father, working three jobs and returning home after
midnight six days a week, had sealed the deal with a $5,000
loan from his younger brother, sweet Uncle Jack, who was still
a bachelor and had that kind of extra cash. I knew that we
owed this money, and every week I would ask my mother at
dinner if it had been paid off in full. How we celebrated at our
small dining room table, toasting each other with our glasses
of juice, when the loan was paid back.

Sometimes my mother and I would watch the courtroom
trial proceedings together, sitting on the rough dark-green
sleeper sofa that still served as my parents' bed. But my memory, perhaps wrong, is that most of the time I sat alone in the
room taking in the enormity of what had happened. Before, I
had known that Jews were murdered in Europe, but I had not
grasped the scale of it.

The trial seemed to go on forever as survivor after survivor
was given the chance to speak, and through testimony could
bear witness and salvage a fistful of justice. From the hours
spent in that world, I believed that I had absorbed the whole
of Adolph Eichmann much the way the whale had swallowed
Jonah. A specific place in my brain seemed to hold the physical
and moral embodiment of Eichmann so that later whenever
I thought of the Holocaust, he stood at the gate to that vast,
unseen world.

As an adult, I saw photographs of the trial and the man himself. Everything I remembered was true, although my memory
had enlarged and exaggerated the features of his face. Eichmann was seated in a glass enclosure along with two guards
standing at his sides like angels in uniform. Thin, dressed in
a loose dark suit, he was mostly bald with a few remaining
strands of hair across his head. He wore glasses with thick

black frames, and bulky headphones covered his ears so he could follow the translated proceedings. His eyes were impassive, seemingly unseeing, and his mouth, set straight, was a black hole that had swallowed six million universes.

Eichmann's expression was devoid of everything, and it was not human. The contrast of his polite, studied stillness—as if he were the guest of honor at a dinner party—with the survivors in the room, their faces twisted in remembrance, seemed a study in the casualness of evil. When he spoke in German, I asked my mother what he was saying. I remember looking at her lovely profile as she stared at the television. "He is saying that he didn't do it," she answered.

And I understood exactly what it was he denied doing. I can still feel the nubs of the coarse fabric of the sofa, how they scratched at my dangling legs as I sat and watched the small black-and-white television. I knew that Eichmann had tried to kill my parents when they were little children, arousing in me the impulse to protect. But my mother and father had been carefully hidden away by their own parents in Russia, far from their homes in Poland, and so Eichmann hadn't found them. Because of this Nazi incompetence, my brother and I had been born. This is what I knew then, at six.

There is something else that has haunted me since, like a golem: the vacuum that was created in the death camps. An absence that imposes itself still and will forever—wavelike onto generations ahead. A void, like a shotgun blast in reverse, that came into being from the unrealized dreams of children who held their mothers' hands as they walked naked into showers that weren't really showers.

The children who survived were changed forever at their most elemental level, their DNA. The terror they experienced shattered their phenotypes—the ways in which their genes were expressed and behaved—and delivered to the next generation an overabundance of fear and anxiety, a predisposition to feel stress when others did not. The light of childhood had been extinguished from my mother when she was six years old, and despite the apparent normalcy I grew up in, after the Eichmann trial I was never able to keep my own innocence alive.

With everything they had, my parents struggled to protect me and my brother. The end of the war had brought with it a rudimentary resolution for my mother and father, and they were not reluctant to talk about what they had seen and undergone. Early on, I understood why they could so easily revisit those years of loss and deprivation. Despite it all, they had won, they had lived. Not only had they survived, but their parents and siblings had as well. Emerging from that place of death with one's family intact was a miracle.

As a child, I urgently read the works of the Holocaust writers, Primo Levi and Simon Wiesenthal. I learned that my constant fears and longing to remake history had been born of my in-absentia experience of the Holocaust. It was a relief to know that the thoughts preoccupying me were shared and expressed by those who had survived. When I read their books, the constant hum of grief that inhabited me lost steam and became funneled into something solid with concrete boundaries—written work about the Holocaust. Reading the authors' ideas and analyses, and most importantly, beginning to understand the historical and psychological context, I started to make sense of what had happened, the "why" of it. The words of these authors resonated through me, and I felt closer to them than to my own peers.

In school, I had known a few children whose parents had lived to see liberation, from a concentration camp, a death march, or after years of hiding in the forest—often as the sole survivor of their family. There seemed to be a secret pact among these survivors not to speak of what had happened to them. Especially to their children. As if the telling could taint their sons and daughters with the stain that still dwelled inside them.

Children might inquire about what had happened to their parents during the war. Turned away, sometimes ungently, the children knew not to ask again. So rather than mental landscapes of emaciated bodies or brick chimneys spewing human ash, their heads were filled with imagined horrors suggested in the tight faces and haunted demeanor of their parents. The power of these visions was unfettered, the lack of explicit explanation making conjured images far more gruesome and dangerous because there could always be more.

But my parents' descriptions were clear, so the images in my mind were precisely defined—but, oh, what I did with those images! Between the telling and retelling, the visions that bloomed from these stories were barely distinguishable from my own imprinted memories. Dreamlike scenes became allegory—narratives that began in warm homes filled with the fragrance of cooking and humming with prayers ushering in the Sabbath but ending in death in Auschwitz or Siberia. I breathed in the memories of my family until they became my own.

One such story was of Chava, my mother's youngest aunt, after whom I was named. Eve is my middle name, and Chava is Hebrew for the Garden of Eden's disgraced first lady. She stood on the selection line after arriving at the Auschwitz train station in the summer of 1942 and went to the gas chamber in Birkenau the same day holding her two-year-old son, Anshel, and the hand of another woman's child.

Was that mother's instinct to survive stronger than any need to hold and comfort her child, no matter what the next stop of their journey might be? Or perhaps she desperately needed to search for another loved one. When I first heard this story, I felt the terror of a child separated from her mother. What could Chava have said to distract the little girl, to comfort her? Perhaps she told her that her mother would return soon, or pointed out the flowers in bloom as they walked toward Birkenau. Or did she say nothing, frozen in her own terror?

I agonized over such stories, and like a punch in the gut that repeats and repeats, they followed me everywhere no matter how hard I tried to rid myself of them. It should have been impossible for me to ponder the agonizing questions of morality invoked by such tales, but ponder—or, rather, obsess—is exactly what I did.

My inheritance of the Holocaust was knitted into the architecture of my mind, and perusing the writings of my heroes, the Nazi hunters, ignited a hunger for retribution. Each Nazi found and brought to justice was a battle won in my war. I imagined myself the apprentice of Simon Wiesenthal, the most famous hunter of all, and fantasized about leaping from my bedroom window into a waiting boat (floating miraculously in my father's vegetable garden below) that would spirit me to South America and down the Amazon where I would find the executioner of my family, Joseph Mengele, burrowed deep in his jungle lair.

By the mid-1960s the war had been over for two decades, but for me it continued, imbuing nearly everything I perceived, felt, or experienced with a life-or-death quality, as if I lived on the edge of a precipice. Manifesting as an unrelenting sense of impending catastrophe, it usually hovered noisily at the very front of my mind, but sometimes I felt it as a low colicky beat of warning against my skin. In my mind, that which was bad would inevitably occur, and tragedy—or forced deportation—lurked just around the next corner.

I was attracted to rather than repelled by disaster, reasoning that I would find it before it found me. This atrophying doctrine had its way with me, steering me toward choices that on the surface seemed reasonable but had not come from a will that was free. Like an oil infused with poisonous herbs, my parents' childhoods had bled into mine. Yet behind the fears, desperate to get out of the way of the frightened child was someone else, brave and strong.

CHAPTER 6

MEMORIES OF EVIL
(THE 1960s)

Fear and vigilance were my childhood companions. Much of the anguish I lived with evolved from the *way* the Holocaust was translated by my child's brain, and how my fears were channeled inward, against myself.

When I was young, I did not think that my dread or ruminations were pathological; I expected to feel these things in a world I knew to be brutal. Fear was a quid pro quo for being alive. I never fully believed that the world was safe simply because the Nazis had been vanquished—I knew that the world had given birth to Nazism and could again. And that is what I always was on alert for. I never considered that there would be mass roundups and concentration camps in America. The aggressions that might come for us would be smaller, subtler, but equally deadly.

By the age of six, I had learned of the Holocaust in its totality, albeit in broad outlines: Jews were hunted in Europe where my parents lived because they/we were not considered human. Six million were killed—shot, burned alive, or shoved naked into gas chambers and then their bodies were burned in massive ovens.

As I matured, I discovered that I had processed the Holocaust in chunks corresponding to stages of my intellectual development. In the beginning, my imaginings were concrete. In my mind's eye, I saw multitudes of people running naked from men in uniform; later I imagined the emotions of the people, the embarrassment over their nakedness, the terror of being separated from their children, their parents, their spouses.

And then I would pore over the pages of the books I read to find some explanation for how the Nazis could so easily kill Jewish children while loving and protecting their own. From these ponderings came the assumption that although the sins were not mine, I was required to do penance in return for living. My penance was the hairpin triggers that, lodged in my mind, could turn pleasure in misery, jubilation into dread. I could live, but peace was carefully curtailed and meted out.

The memories that I had co-opted were transformed into signposts pointing in ever more perilous directions. If my mother was late to pick me up from school, it was because she was distracted and a car had struck and killed her. Or, once again careless, she had been kidnapped by the man who parked his car in front of our house. If my parents were out together at night, I would become convinced I would never see them again because they were unthinkingly carefree and would crash their car. My anxiety grew until it had become a near frenzy when they finally came home. A serial killer who made the front page of the newspaper would soon be at our door.

The content of my fears changed as I grew, but they were always there in some form. Usually my imaginings involved catastrophes that would befall us because I was off guard. Much like my mother and her need to know her parents' location during the war, I was a vigilant child. But what I also had to know was what was unsaid, what my parents might be keeping from me. The way my grandfather Abe had orchestrated his family's survival had likely given my mother ample reason to keep certain information from her children.

My father was a gentle and straightforward man, and I do not believe that he had an emotional investment in keeping things from us. The household of his youth had been free and boisterous, with his uncles creating youthful havoc at his parents' home. Although my father's parents, Edmund and Regina, had also fled to Russian-held territory from their home in Poland, Edmund had managed to avoid the deportation of his family to Siberia.

My father's wartime experiences had been far less virulent than those of my mother, and I cleaved to his lightness and the joyful spirit that the war had not taken from him. While my mother worried about any lurking menace, my dad laughed and joked and played. Because of his love of literature and classical music, our living room was lined with books, modern and ancient, and filled with the strains of Chopin, Tchaikovsky, Mozart, and for dessert, the waltzes of Strauss. Rock and roll was curiously foreign to my parents, but still my dad would lift my little brother horizontally and, strumming on Steve's belly, pretend my giggling brother was a guitar. Then bending his knees to the sides like Beatle John, my dad would break into the hit song of the day, singing, "She loves you, yeah, yeah, YEAH!"

He had us in stitches, and to that end he was always willing to play the clown. My father was deeply intelligent. We would call him our encyclopedia and, in later years, our own Google. We clamored to know about his much-vaunted princely life before the war.

Photographs showed my father to be a beautiful, serious, full-cheeked child looking confidently into the camera, frequently dressed in velvet like a Little Lord Fauntleroy. He told us of the scholar he had been as a youngster and that by necessity he was pushed ahead several grades. With a deep and mischievous pride, my father boasted about reading Tolstoy's *Anna Karenina* in the prerevolutionary Russian Cyrillic text at the age of nine. But it was the open beauty of his heart that drew so many to him, and I cannot remember my father's heart ever being closed to the world.

He wanted to learn as much as possible, and he embraced what was unknown, exhilarated by the process of mastering anything new. His green eyes seemed perpetually lit in a joyful fever of living. It was my father who bore responsibility for infusing me with the ability to feel the exuberance and joy I managed to eke out of my early years.

My mother was more concerned with our physical well-being, of which her family had been so uncertain during the years of war. It was not that she was emotionally ungenerous—she gave with all she had *if* she believed it was what we needed. Like Maslow's hierarchy of needs, my mother often could not imagine that we had needs beyond the physical. And it was only when we were safe that she could rest.

My father's family had not been forced to travel into Siberia, remaining only at its periphery, and had not been brutalized by cold and hunger during the war; I don't recall my father ever speaking of physical discomfort. So, when I was still a pre-teen, and my mother simply could not understand why I *had* to have those white vinyl go-go boots with the zipper up the back, or the chunky navy patent leather Mary Janes, my father moved in— gently, mindful of her feelings. I would skip along, reaching up to hold my father's index finger in my fist as we slipped away to the inexpensive shoe store in the shopping center a mile away. This store did not sell the carefully made shoes for children's tender growing bones my mother preferred, but rather stocked the fabulous trends of the sixties. These outings with my father made my mom pretend to frown but were my delight.

The war had taught my mother different things about survival, things my father miraculously did not have to learn. When my grandmother Rose pushed her bread at her children, Lusia had felt it impossible that her mother was not hungry, and she learned that love could be delivered wrapped in a fiction. And certainly, truth is not always absolute; a mother's own hunger can recede in the face of her child's.

I often felt that what my mother was thinking was different from what her words conveyed. The dissonance between what she said and what I believed to be true became a familiar experience and a precursor to the distrust that often characterized and harmed the important relationships of my life. I think my mother simply believed that love was not connected to communication. She usually spoke with unusual forthrightness, but in matters of protecting her loved ones, she did not feel it was necessary—more likely, it was a hindrance—to getting the job done.

And once everyone was safe, why would it matter that my mother's logistics had not involved explanations? Abe made the decisions that saved the lives of his family, and he neither consulted them nor sought their opinions. Perhaps my mother might have seen her parents involve others in decisions more democratically had the war not broken apart their lives. But her childhood ended at the age of six, and I believe that my mother saw authority as the only way to parent.

My mother's reticence to explain, to share, and to openly discuss family problems or crises made me wonder what brewed behind the scenes. I developed a fierce need to gauge what people felt and thought. When my mother hid her thoughts from me, it scared me, triggering catastrophic scenarios. After all, I knew from my parents' own childhood experiences that adults planned for looming threats. I learned to look carefully for signs that there was more behind my mother's words: eyes that were averted, tight facial expressions, and a quality to her voice that allowed for little discussion.

To my mother's dismay, I often demanded to know the truth. A frequent refrain of mine was "What are you *not* telling me!" My mother was often reluctant to verbalize her feelings when she feared they would be rejected or misunderstood, and I developed skills to listen for what was not conveyed verbally. This became a double-edged sword later in my own relationships because I could not accept words at face value and I gave more weight to what I felt the person was feeling than to what was said. Sometimes it is not possible to know *exactly* what one feels at a moment in time, yet I would *demand* that they know.

When I think of my mother's parents, their single-minded efforts to keep their children alive and then their unimaginable losses, I marvel that they had not been wholly destroyed by the war. But part of them had split apart and died. In contrast to the decimation of my mother's family, my father's parents, Edmund and Regina, had not lost a single child, sister, brother, nephew, or niece, and for them life still held promise. But Rose and Abe had lost too many to return to the people they had been. For where does one's love, and the energy that fuels that love, go when half of the dyad is orphaned?

When a beloved disappears, the identity of the person who is left—the one who is no longer called Mother or Father or Sister or Aunt—is changed. It untethers from the core of the self but still drifts on in a state of mourning, an unrelieved ache. I learned this for myself many years later when my son left. Who was I when he was gone? The tie had been disconnected but still hovered, always reminding me of his absence, and who I no longer was in relation to him. But my son was alive and breathing. Not alongside me, but he breathed, and hope for a different future was a powerful salve for my loss.

There was no such hope for Abe and Rose—no goodbye, no final embrace, no burial rites to close the wound, just empty space where the beloved had once been. For me, the measure of every wrenching loss always returns to the losses of the Holocaust, the touchstone by which I calibrate grief.

My grandfather Edmund could feel what was coming as Abe had. He was pragmatic and confident, well-educated, and spoke German as well as Polish and Yiddish. Edmund went to synagogue infrequently but knew the prayers of his Ashkenazi forebears. He was a businessman, a talented entrepreneur who had married well. Regina was dark-haired and butter-skinned, a young woman of such incandescent beauty that in their engagement photograph her sublime oval face and heavy-lidded eyes dared the viewer to look away.

Edmund and Regina lived in a small city not far from Krakow and were prosperous factory owners before the Nazi invasion. When they fled, they traveled in cars toward the eastern border until their vehicles were commandeered by the Soviet army.

For my father and his younger brother, Jack, the war was almost an adventure. I think Edmund and Regina's ability to survive the Holocaust and later reinvent themselves in America was due partly to their optimistic mindset, but more crucially, it pivoted on one factor—they had been spared the loss of any member of their immediate family. Their losses were only material.

With deep pride in his voice, my grandfather Edmund had confided to me that unlike all the other women in the Soviet labor camp, his wife did not have to work, which was nearly unheard-of. There, my grandmother Regina did what I had always known her to do. She cooked, not the dandelion soup of my mother's wartime dinners, but real food—meat, potatoes, and vegetables found who knows where. Though my father never mentioned being hungry in Russia, I could recite from memory the words my mother used to describe nights she fought the pain in her empty belly. But the tales my father told were funny, even uplifting.

When my grandfather Edmund broke his leg, my dad, at fourteen, replaced him at his work, managing a farm. With laughing eyes, he talked of collecting cow manure that would be used for fuel, how he would run over with his bucket whenever a cow's tail began to twitch. And there was the time thieves dumped sleeping powder on him and his brother Jack and ransacked the place while the boys slept. They woke to find themselves covered with hundreds of feathers freed from pillows. The thieves had cut them open searching for the valuables they were certain were hidden in the home of my grandfather Edmund, a man who still wore his homburg hat in a world that had forgotten grace.

But the war had incinerated nearly everything Rose and Abe cherished, and the sum total of their grief was greater than any part of them left unwounded. There was a great disconnect between the man I knew growing up and the myth that surrounded my grandfather Abe. He was a handsome, charming man who had lived an ordinary life before the war. He had always been a force of will, but the war had forged a giant. I wish I had seen that man.

Despite everything that should have torn his faith from his heart, Abe remained deeply religious and prayed daily. He mediated between his wife and daughters when necessary and would sit at his living room window in New York for hours in silence, gazing outside. By the time I was born in 1955, my mother's parents had made their permanent home in a drab brick building in Sunnyside, an industrial area of Queens whose bleak topography belied its name. When my grandfather sat at his window with a small glass of whiskey and the Yiddish newspaper, he gave the impression of admiring a lovely vista rather than the ugly backsides of buildings built on lots so tiny they appeared to be part of one mangled whole.

Abe's English was limited, the language of his soul being Yiddish, and we did not speak much to each other. But I would sit close to him, listening to the melodies he half sang, half hummed in a low voice graveled by years of smoking. My mother said the songs were melodies his mother had sung to him when he was a child. He and I did not play or laugh as I did with my father's parents. I suspected that it was emotional fatigue that had caused Abe to simply run dry, with just left-over bits for his grandchildren. After all, we had been *born*. Abe had saved his daughters, they had become mothers, and his work was done. At his window in Queens, my grandfather's peaceful gaze told me that the brick and steel view was beautiful but framed in heartbreak.

I could feel the sadness everywhere in their home—in the subdued furnishings of their apartment, the quiet colors my grandmother wore, the downward pull of her face, and the slumped posture of my grandfather at the window seat. They both seemed to exist in the shadows cast by memories of the ones they had loved and still longed for—memories that dwindled every year. Rose would lament the absence of photographs of her parents: "If I only had one—just one—picture of my mother so I could see her sweet face again." Photos were all left behind when they fled.

Abe expressed his grief through anger. When he first learned that his brother, Mehul, had been killed in front of his synagogue by a neighbor who wanted his house, Abe's rage nearly propelled him back to Poland with the intent of killing this man. He was stopped only by the pleadings of his wife and daughters.

Rose said, "No, Avrum. Leave him to God." Abe listened to her.

My grandmother lived to be 101, her memory clear, crowded to the end with her brothers and sisters and their children at the gates of hell. In the hospital, my mother at her side, Rose spoke in Yiddish, "*S'iz shoyn genug.*" It's enough already.

CHAPTER 7

LOOKING AT THE WORLD WITH JO
(THE 1960s)

O ur home in Queens had been the least expensive house in the neighborhood. It was pretty and compact, with swings in the back yard and a large oak tree in the front. Inside our house I felt cloistered but not safe. The anxiety pent up inside me spilled over, ready to taint anything I encountered. Sometimes I felt as if my life were a stage play directed by a deranged curator of memories behind whom stood the ghosts of Auschwitz.

My father had built bookshelves in our small living room and filled them with hardbacks from his book-of-the-month club. The dust covers were colorful illustrations that beckoned seductively, and I followed them into unimagined places. When I was not reading the testimony of Holocaust survivors, my favorite authors were H. G. Wells, Sidney Taylor, Pearl S. Buck, and Anya Seton. They gave me a perspective of history less insular than the one I was accustomed to.

H. G. Wells showed me new and fantastic worlds. I fell in love with Sidney Taylor's Jewish family in turn-of-the-century New York. Hers were the first books I read with Jewish characters. Pearl S. Buck's searing tales of peasants starving and laboring in Chinese rice fields broke my heart. And when I read Anya Seton, I was a fly on the walls of King Edward's court, Katherine of Aragon's castle, and Governor John Winthrop's home.

That I read the classics was critical to my father, and as a reward for reading Dickens, Steinbeck, and Dreiser, which he plucked from the highest shelves, he gave me *Gone with the Wind*. Its dog-eared pages were smeared purple from the pistachio nuts I fiendishly ate during my twelfth summer. I kept my books stacked across both sides of my bed on a pair of night tables, part of a fancy gold-and-white painted bedroom set Edmund and Regina had bought for my eighth birthday. Nothing compared to the euphoria I felt ensconced in bed with my books around me.

My library card was my portal to a world not shaped by the Holocaust, and I would carry my borrowed books ten blocks to our house, five or six of them in each arm. They were my treasures, and I read several at once. But I was inherently careless and usually returned the books late, having filled my pockets with pilfered change to pay the overdue fees.

The librarian would take the money from me with a disappointed expression. After a couple of years of this, she stopped lecturing me about my behavior. She developed some sympathy for me when I asked her once to speak to my father. He had insisted I read *The Last of the Mohicans* by James Fenimore Cooper, which I found too dense and difficult to get through. He threatened to withhold other books until I finished it. The librarian explained to my father that there were more appropriate choices for a child. He listened to her, and I was so relieved and grateful to the librarian that I brought my library books back on time for the next few months.

Most of the neighbors on our street had interests foreign to my parents, including baseball, which was big in our neighborhood. The fathers watched games on TV, and their sons played ball on the street. My dad had no comprehension of baseball or its appeal until my brother grew up enough to explain the game to him. My father would take Steve to see the Mets while lugging the whole Sunday edition of the *New York Times* on the subway so as not to be caught in the frightening position of having nothing to read during the long ordeal.

At home, my parents played my father's classical music LP records on our stereo. Most things in our home were second-hand, and the "hi-fi" was one of the few possessions they had bought new.

My mother was my friend, and I was hers. We shared only a slight interest in cultivating friendships with others. I always felt a distance, made up of history and culture, between me and other girls. I was envious of them, their American-ness, their Christmas and Easter celebrations, their carefree personas, never having had to consider the unlikely odds of being born. With other Jewish children, I could not wrap my head around their lack of angst, their fearlessness, the way they took for granted the privileged American lives they led.

I think my mother felt a similar disconnect with her peers, although we never spoke about it until I was an adult. She did not expect the housewives who lived on our block to understand the experiences that had made up her early life. My mother could no more envision a childhood free of trauma blossoming deliciously into adolescence than these women could imagine sleeping on the cold ground for months at a time or sheltering from the whistling of bombs that fell from the sky. How could they understand not bathing for half a decade, or the sensation of immersing, finally, into the glorious warmth of a bath only to burn with humiliation as lice fell into the water? My mother and these women were simply too strange to each other, and neighbors rarely approached her.

Lusia's name had been Americanized to Lucy, and her social life in America consisted of family—her husband, her sister, and her parents—and the few friends from Poland who had also survived the war. My mother was beautiful, with blue eyes and heavy dark hair that fell past her shoulders. She had the kind of unconcerned beauty that drew envy from women and overtures from men. I was proud because when she came to school for a teacher meeting or class play, she was the prettiest and youngest mother. My father said he was stopped in his tracks when he saw her for the first time on the train in Europe.

Until I was twelve, I had few friends. Other children recognized a heaviness in me, a chip on my shoulder that was off-putting. Much of my internal world was made up of what I had not experienced, and this created great discord with my daily life as a child in Queens.

If the lost world of my murdered family came alive as I read the stories of war in my father's books, I also gained an identity that straddled my actual childhood existence and my phantom life, as if I existed in two dimensions at once. Seated at my scratched wooden desk crammed with pencils and notebooks and crayons, I felt alien in the classroom, a different species. Invariably something I was taught would connect to my parents' wartime experiences and I would be in Poland in 1939 or Auschwitz in 1942. Visions of past and present juxtaposed in my mind, and though distinct, I could not keep the images separate as the emotions they evoked bled together. It seemed inconceivable that I sat safely in class when other Jewish children a mere generation before had spent their last moments of life on selection lines. And the layers upon layers of images and sensations blurred together, stripping me of my ability to reason them away.

In retrospect, I think that my difficulty in maintaining friendships with other children came from believing that true connection would never be possible because of our vast differences in background. I felt this way with both non-Jews and Jews whose parents were not survivors. The strongest sense of who I was came from an inhumane past that I had not lived.

I felt that my physical world in school—on the playground, at a birthday party— lacked seriousness and seemed to be a bubble-like fairyland where children were well fed, had pretty clothes and toys, and were not hunted. Later, when I outgrew elementary school, I encountered other children whose parents had survived, and with them I felt a new sense of ease as if I had removed a heavy brace.

And then a miracle happened on my first day of junior high school. It was there I met Jo. She was small-boned, with large brown doe eyes and dark-blond hair like silk, which she would straighten by rolling it around a juice can on top of her head. A deadpan manner fronted her hilarious and devilish sense of humor. We fit the places in each other that had been roughed out by parents whose focus was elsewhere. In many ways, Jo saved my life.

We found each other with the force of lovers who had been separated across eons of time and oceans of distance. Indeed, the magical possibilities of reincarnation came to be an enduring theme in our thirteen-year-old minds. We would spend hours on Jo's bed in her narrow room trying to hypnotize each other. We modeled our efforts on *The Search for Bridey Murphy*, a book published in 1956 about a Midwestern housewife who, during psychoanalysis, spoke of her life as a young woman in nineteenth-century Ireland, and then of yet another life, as an infant in New Amsterdam who did not survive to her second year. We were obsessed with this idea, and using the book as our guide, practiced methods of hypnosis it described, hoping to find lives we, too, had lived before. Each of us, in turn, lay on the bed while the other would intone in a low, dramatic voice, "You are so tired; you cannot move. Your hand is getting heavier and heavier. It weighs a thousand pounds, and you couldn't move it if you tried."

It was the late 1960s, disenfranchised people who had been pushed for decades to the margins of society were rebelling, and Jo and I were transported by these social and political upheavals. New information hurtled around in our growing brains, processed through prisms of innocence and wonder. We would grab our bicycles, race to our meeting place, and spend our days exploring. Everything seemed new and untouched, but when we were fourteen, boys found Jo, and their attentions brought her a solace that I could not give her. I grieved when I was supplanted by her first boyfriend, Jeff, whom she met at our Zionist youth group.

Boys began to flock to Jo, but as an adolescent, I felt unnatural trying to navigate the rules of dating, and I could not manage the new terrain. I would be left sometimes, afterward, with what felt tantamount to physical debris, and it was impossible to know if the pain was leaning on my mind or my body—I just knew I was deeply uncomfortable.

Calmness in others was strange to me. People would ask about the earnest expression on my face and what it meant. Boys I liked would say I was "intense." I never took it as a compliment, though it might have been. I felt it meant I was too much work, and I wished I could be lighter and more nonchalant like the girls who flirted as if it were an organic ability. They seemed to make the boys so happy.

When I was seventeen and camping out with friends on a freezing beach in the Sinai, I had a crush on a boy in our group. He was skinny and angelic-looking, with blue eyes and messy blond curls. I was so excited when he approached me.

Offering me a puff of the joint he held, he said with a friendly but awful finality, "You really are deep, aren't you?"

As far as I understood then, these words were a death knell, and I learned to tone down my reactions, imitating those who were quieter and, I thought, more palatable to others. Of course, when I was safe with my family, emotional intensity was the norm and a huge source of pride. At home, I would have been sent to the hospital if I had tamped down my expressions.

I liked to draw as a kid, and my grandfather Edmund, seeing me use anything I could get my hands on, would bring reams of letterhead paper from work. I dreamed of becoming a fashion designer and applied to art school. We traveled from Queens to Manhattan for the "audition."

It was a wet, snowy March day, and my mother and I walked through brown slush on the edge of Central Park. I was scared that I would be turned down, found wanting. The talent in that school was enormous, and for the first time, I was not the best artist in the room. The artwork on display was new to my eyes: people who did not look like people, undefined with edges that merged into other people or objects. This expressionistic art challenged my thinking. My talent immediately felt mediocre, and I had no use for that. I was intimidated by the other students, awed not just because of their gifts that seemed endless, but by their openness to everything new.

The year was 1969, and the autumn I started art school followed the Summer of Love and Woodstock. Long-haired boys and girls in jeans that dragged on the ground were getting high on the school steps. I was tantalized but ultimately too frightened to participate. I had to put myself on the outside of the excitement lest I be swept along. I had to stay alert, and because Jo was not with me, it was difficult. I transferred to my neighborhood high school, and except for a couple of college art classes, I did not draw again.

CHAPTER 8

REFUGEES IN AMERICA (THE 1960s)

A s the first grandchild born in the United States and the only girl, I was given favored status by my grandparents and savored every minute of it. After my mother and father, my paternal grandparents Edmund and Regina were my dearest loves. They threw off joy like starlight.

When I was in elementary school, we took trips together, saw movies and shows, and visited their friends from Europe who were also happy. In his new life, my grandfather worked as a salesman for a large appliance store in Queens. His intellect and precise knowledge of the televisions and stereo systems he sold made him a favorite with customers.

He and I understood each other, and we could talk for hours. I often stayed overnight in their small apartment, which was a short bus and subway ride from our house. It was warm and lovely and my grandmother fed me incessantly while she taught me how to cook. The apartment faced the street and was radiant from the sun and filled with the aromas of my grandmother's schnitzel and brisket and fried chicken and potato latkes, all swimming in butter, still years away from the cholesterol panic.

We would hike down to Queens Boulevard, my grandmother wearing high heels and pushing her metal shopping cart purposefully in front of her, chatting with neighbors while I forced my shorter legs to keep up. I could not wait, so we usually stopped first at the tiny, crammed toy store and then on to the butcher, finishing up at the supermarket.

When we returned home, Regina cooked and I helped her bake and then feasted on what we had made. After dinner, I would browse through my grandparents' treasure trove—their collection of Broadway show albums: *South Pacific, My Fair Lady, The Sound of Music, The Music Man, The King and I.* I found the album covers to be works of art, and I remember them still. Given the responsibility of operating the record player on my own, I remember aiming the needle carefully toward the correct groove so as not to scratch the record, and feeling the rush of delight as the music burst forth.

Regina would wait to eat her dinner with my grandfather when he returned from work, after nine o'clock in the evening. I was always thrilled when he would stride confidently through the door and I could finally tell him about all the adventures of the day. Edmund listened thoughtfully to everything with great interest, offering thoughts and commenting approvingly on what we had purchased at the toy store.

I would sit with my grandparents at the polished dining table, sometimes eating a second dinner or just nibbling at my grandmother's crispy but tender golden brown potato *latkes* as I listened to them speaking in Polish. Edmund was perfectly fluent in English, but Regina never gained comfort with her new language. By then I could understand rudimentary Polish, as it was my parents' default language whenever they wanted privacy from me and my brother. I could follow most of my grandmother's good-natured gossip about her sister or brother, and of course, the price fluctuations at the supermarket.

Edmund was not a humorous man; he did not tell jokes or laugh a great deal as my father did. But he always seemed deeply satisfied with the way his family's life in America had evolved. There was no melancholy spirit surrounding my father's parents, either pushed down or blatant, and with them I felt like a normal child. Without any conscious thought, they led me to focus on the small and innocent delights of childhood.

Tuesdays were my grandfather's day off, and occasionally I would play hooky from school and spend the day with him and my grandmother. They would come to collect me and we'd make the trip into Manhattan to Radio City Music Hall. We sat in plush red velvet seats as the orchestra in its pit rose up amid a glamorous smoke effect. The Rockette dancers performed in a show that was followed by a newly released film. We were the three musketeers, and I lived for the days we spent together.

Apprehension of America and its culture did not seem to exist for Edmund and Regina. My father's parents were different from other survivors; they never appeared to look over their shoulders for that invisible threat. Their new world in America had color and beauty and they loved it, embracing everything that was foreign at first. Their television was the newest model, they subscribed to *Life* and *Look* magazines, and they vacationed in Miami Beach. Regina and I watched together as the Beatles performed on her favorite television program, the *Ed Sullivan Show*. We also watched movies on the color television; Regina was enamored of Hollywood's leading men and ladies—Elizabeth Taylor, Marilyn Monroe, Gregory Peck, Jean Simmons, and Tyrone Power were her favorites. She always seemed to have the latest information about them, including the state of their marriages.

My grandparents had 1960s *Mad Men*–style accessories. Cigarette lighters, frosted highball glasses, and modern electrical appliances and gadgets were spread throughout the apartment. The heavy European crystal glassware and china they favored was kept safely away from my notoriously clumsy fingers in a tall oak hutch.

After immigrating to the U.S., Edmund and Regina had swiftly become American in terms of loyalty, outlook, and consumption. They became citizens in the early 1950s, yet they and the other relatives were still known as "greeners." The unflattering term described their earliest status in the United States, marking those who sought refuge in a new country and were "green" (as in new and unformed). But I also heard my relatives use the word to refer to themselves. I thought *greener* was an ironic term, and if my family members used it first, the description could inure them to possible rejection by those who were "real Americans." More than once I heard someone respond to the sound of my mother's accent by muttering, "Why don't you go back where you came from!"

Her reply was a well-crafted and laconic, "And I suppose you came here on the *Mayflower*? You look old enough."

The men in my family, having been educated in Europe, now found work in clothing factories or tailoring shops. They made the transition from prosperous, tolerated Jews to manual laborers in textile industries or in the dusty back rooms of department stores. But I have no memory of hearing complaints; rather, whenever we gathered there was laughter, interesting cursing in Polish and Yiddish, and teasing that was generally affectionate but could also bite. Like the time the stock market went down and my great-uncle Dolek gave my great-uncle Schnapps a nasty ribbing for his stock choices: "Oy, Schnapps! I vould haff killed myself if I lost as much money as you did in the mahket!"

Except for Edmund and Rose, both of whom read the *New York Times* every day, my relatives' command of English never grew beyond what was needed to shop, travel on public transportation, or work at a job with little face-to-face contact with the public. The women cared for their small apartments with an ardor that came from having lost and then regained a home. They cleaned and polished, cooked and baked in the dense Eastern European style of the kitchens they had known as children.

My father's side of the family, having had the luck to survive the war losing only things rather than loved ones, were a fun, generous lot. At countless gatherings, the great-aunts and uncles stretched the length of Regina's long dining table, which could, in a flash, be transformed into a card table for an impromptu game of poker after dinner.

Before the war Edmund had been a manufacturer of party goods near the city of Krakow. He was also an inventor. Sitting cross-legged on the carpet of my grandparents' living room, I would fiddle with the small, tarnished silver contraption I found in a chest next to the plastic-sheathed sofa. My grandfather explained it was a scale that could distinguish counterfeit from genuine coins. How Edmund had managed to have the device patented was a genuine mystery.

On New Year's Eve, my grandparents' friends would pile into their apartment. I remember parties that seemed lit by accelerant, vibrating with laughter, ice cubes clinking in tall, gold-frosted glasses. The bed was piled high with coats that shed bits of their owners—perfume, an errant hair, a lipstick smudge—along with whatever fur was reasonably priced that year. The fur coats were my favorite and made for a soft landing under my jumping feet.

During Passover, Regina baked a flourless torte of chopped nuts layered between coffee buttercream and iced with dark chocolate. Her sister and sister-in-law stood guard by the torte in the tiny galley kitchen until it was time to slice and serve, and then woe to the fool (usually my father) who asked for seconds as the women quickly divided the remaining cake among themselves. These pieces were packed in foil with frightening speed and disappeared, leaving the rest of us stunned with our plates emptied of every crumb, the taste still lingering on the tongue, a memory to be cherished until the next year.

My grandparents' sofa was an extra-long affair with twin oak side tables attached at both ends. The drawers of these tables contained treasures, artifacts that wed their pre-war lives to the present. Theirs had not been the limited world of the country shtetl; my father's family were sophisticated city dwellers. My father would tease my mother, saying that she came from a long line of peasants.

In the drawers, I found photographs in tones of gray and cream that showed elegant men and women strolling on cobblestone streets or picnicking on riverbanks. The expressions on the faces of my father's parents and aunts and uncles were usually jaunty, a well-nurtured sense of contentment coming through as they proudly wore the accoutrements of 1930s European bourgeois society: fur-trimmed coats, elegant suits, and hats with netting. They held walking sticks or umbrellas as they posed in front of shiny dark automobiles. And there were images of laughing partygoers in costume, and scenes of verdant summers in southern Poland, the happy vacationers leaning in together for the photographer.

Nowhere in these images were hints of a world about to be annihilated. The photos were set in gold tabs on ecru pages in cracked leather albums; they were never left loose. Souvenirs from excursions to the Statue of Liberty, the United Nations, and Jones Beach were scattered companionably alongside the photo albums. In the same drawer, there were brochures of

fancy Miami Beach hotels. The edges of the enticing advertise-
ments of wavy-haired girls tossing red beach balls to unseen
partners were frayed from my constant handling. Inside the
brochures were shots of the various hotel ballrooms, theaters,
swimming pools, and underground shopping promenades.
Also in the drawer were older brochures from Edmund's long-
gone factory with hand-drawn pictures of party favors, hats,
and twirling noisemakers on flimsy, almost translucent paper.

What did this collection of artifacts say about the internal struggle of my paternal grandparents? The objects of a lost
world were nestled alongside those embodying the American
ideals of freedom, safety, and prosperity. Were they a seamless
coming together or an attempt to push away the horrors of the
past? The artifacts of both worlds appeared to live together in
Edmund and Regina's drawer as comfortably as their past and
present lives intertwined in their minds. Not only had they
survived, they had thrived after the Holocaust. And in freeing
themselves from the horror of where they had been, they gave
me a semblance of a normal childhood. They insisted on being
free Americans, and I was their free American grandchild. It
felt sometimes like an unholy alliance, and I had trouble rec-
onciling how much memory may have been lost in gaining
freedom.

Edmund and Regina's truth was concealed somewhere
among the items tucked away in the drawers, but as I examined the keepsakes, I wondered about the millions of other
items that had been looted from their frightened owners in
their final hours. The Jews deported to Auschwitz and other
death camps had been given strict instructions on what they
could carry with them. Families stuffed their valises with clothing, shoes, jewelry, photographs, teddy bears, all of which were
taken away when they arrived at the camp. The Nazis would
ransack through the confiscated suitcases which, thrown to

the ground, had formed hills near the railroad tracks. They reasoned that if the deportees were told to bring their belongings, they would not imagine that they were to be killed upon arrival.

What had these objects meant to the victims? What were the occasions memorialized by them and what were the memories contained within their edges? A silver jewelry box from a husband to a wife, a porcelain doll from a mother to a daughter, a set of silverware or embroidered linens from parents to a newly married couple. There would be no grandchildren born of these victims to trace the contours of their beloved treasures.

I have been engaged in a lifelong struggle to not just comprehend intellectually the scope of the Holocaust, but to *feel it*. My failure to do so elicits enormous guilt, but as much as I try to viscerally absorb the scope of genocide, it has been nearly impossible to do so. The remove seems physical, but of course it's not. I was not there, and there is no book, or film, or visit to Auschwitz that could transmit the actual terror of the victims. If I inch closer to the brutal images that reside permanently in my head, of being *in* the gas chamber, I touch a vaulted blackness emptied of every particle of light, and the cells of my body threaten to combust. And I recoil, retreating just as I do when I imagine my baby cousin Barry dying alone. If I could restructure the shape of time and space, I would go back to find Barry in his crib, breathe oxygen into his lungs, and watch his color turn from blue to living pink.

I had no such fantasy of rescuing one and a half million children from death because the number is so vast that I cannot touch the meaning of it. I can try to work it out: There were about thirty children in my classroom each year in elementary school. We were all between the ages of five and twelve—the ages of the children, along with those who were younger, who were immediately gassed because they were too young to work.

That would be 50,000 classrooms of thirty children or 2,500 elementary schools the size of mine. It doesn't matter how I do the math; I can only imagine one child at a time being pushed into a concrete room that within minutes would be filled with lethal gas. And in my mind's eye I see the living child become inanimate—a corpse. Barry has become the proxy for those murdered children in my heart and in my mind.

In 1955 I was born from the primordial stew of a newly regressed civilization, and I instilled in myself an imperative to experience as much of the pain and terror of the murdered as I could. My reasoning was simple. Since I had, against the worst of odds, been born, I must experience emotionally what the six million had lived.

A vision of my mother's aunt Chava on the selection line at Auschwitz holding her baby Anshel and the hand of another woman's child would sometimes come to my mind. To fully comprehend the magnitude of the Holocaust, I had to multiply these three human beings by the millions of others murdered in torment, and then finally to consider the infinite number of their unborn descendants. The extermination of Chava and the two children were heartbreaking symbols of a void of humanity that would follow the Holocaust forever—a world empty of their progeny. This was the void that had haunted me since I saw Adolph Eichmann stand trial on television.

But I needed to keep this pain from becoming visceral and all-consuming. I had to put it away, far down where I could not access it, where the anguish could be transformed into something that I could bear. I believe my obsessive thoughts were the result of this process, probably exacerbated by a genetic predisposition. As excruciating as the ruminations had been at times, they were less horrific than comprehending the magnitude of the wholesale extermination of human beings—members of my extended family.

Edmund and Regina never spoke of such things. Perhaps their natural hopefulness and embrace of life allowed them to turn away from a homeland that had betrayed them and toward the one that had welcomed them, the one whose shores they would never leave.

CHAPTER 9

NIGHTMARE
(1969)

It was the end of the final year of a turbulent decade. I was fourteen, and my father and I would discuss books or just chat in the morning as he prepared to commute to the Bronx where he worked as an elevator designer. Our black cat Tiger would join us, and after my father left, I usually had another hour to read and sneak a peanut butter and jelly sandwich before breakfast; my appetite was legendary in our home.

On a morning late in November, I woke up early—just past sunrise. My father was doing his calisthenics, and as was my habit, I sat on the floor of the living room and we laughed as Tiger jumped on my father's back while he did his pushups. At 6:30 he walked out the door and to the corner of our street where he would cross the wide avenue to catch his bus to the subway, the first leg of the long trip.

I climbed the stairs to my bedroom, which was the entire second floor of the house. Settling back into bed with my book, I looked at the clock and was delighted to see I had forty-five minutes before I had to dress for school. A scream of metal grinding on metal flew into the room through the window. I jolted upright and the thought *Daddy's been hit* came to me almost parenthetically. I ran down the stairs to the front door and waited. Less than a minute later there was a knock at the door. It was a man—disheveled, florid, scared.

"I just hit your father," he said breathlessly. "He was running."

Then my mother appeared in her nightgown. Her voice seemed to be octaves higher than normal. "Where?" she said.

"He was running, for the bus, maybe? I didn't see him. He's on Hillside Avenue. Someone called an ambulance."

How sorry I felt later for this man. "Is he alive?" I asked, raising my voice to be heard over my mother's keening.

"He's conscious," the man said, the most beautiful words I had ever heard in my life.

In my new pink quilted robe, I tore out of the house barefoot, the skin of my soles sticking to the freezing concrete of the sidewalk. There, in the middle of the four-lane avenue, sat my father. People stood around him, and it seemed like someone had arranged him, propped him up; his limbs looked so odd. One of his legs was not visible.

He's paralyzed, I thought and pictured my strong father jogging and laughingly telling stories of the dogs who chased him. He looked at me. I didn't touch him. His face begged forgiveness.

Then my mother came, also in a robe. "Go back home, take care of your brother!"

I could not move.

"Now!" she yelled.

I ran. At the house, I explained to my nine-year-old brother what had happened and said our father would be well taken care of at the hospital. He would be fine, I told Steve.

My mother was back in the house now, pulling on clothes and speaking half syllables to her reflection in the bathroom mirror. Then she was gone.

Marek Damaszek was my grandparents' friend from Poland. He was a doctor, and my mother called him from the hospital phone booth for guidance. Marek was a sensitive man and called me a few times that day.

I asked, "How is he?"

He responded calmly, almost languidly, "Oh, he's fine, you know—walking around the hospital." But Marek was being kind.

The truth was that my father was in and out of consciousness at a seriously underfunded municipal hospital. They did not take X-rays until my mother screamed at the staff that my father was urinating blood. She asked the resident doctor what could be done to stop the hemorrhaging, and the gentle young man looked at her with limpid, sympathetic eyes and said that my father's lung had been punctured by a broken rib and had collapsed.

"But what are you *doing* for him?" my mother asked, her voice scaling up.

"Maybe you should pray," the doctor said.

Wordlessly, my mother turned away from him and called Dr. Damaszek again. He instructed her to get my father to a hospital in Brooklyn where his surgeon friend would be waiting. But the municipal hospital would not provide an ambulance. It wasn't their policy to transfer a patient to another facility, the hospital administrator told my mother. He said it would be a mistake to move him.

"But no one is treating him!" she said and went back to the telephone booth. Flipping through the thin pages of the heavy phone directory chained to a shelf, she called private ambulance companies and begged. Each one refused until the fifth call.

The dispatcher agreed to transport my father. "You got fifty dollars, lady?" he asked.

"Of course!" she shot back. My mother had left the house without her purse but did not give her lie another thought until they arrived at the destination in Brooklyn. There, she promised the irate driver she would mail a check, which she did a few days later when she began to breathe normally again.

At the hospital in Brooklyn, the surgeon, Dr. Charles Friedgood, waited with his tools in the room my father was wheeled into. There was no time for anesthesia. The surgeon pushed his scalpel between two of my father's ribs, inserted one end of a long rubber tube into the incision, and dropped the other end into a bucket on the floor. Soon, the bucket filled with my father's blood, and his lung began to work again. The surgeon was satisfied and predicted, "He will be fine. He'll need a few weeks of rest, but he will recover."

My father did recover and lived nearly a half century more.

A few years later, Dr. Friedgood, a husband and father, was arrested at the airport on his way to reunite with his Danish nurse, with whom he also had two children. Soon afterward, he was convicted of murdering his wife. The man who had saved my father spent nearly the rest of his life in prison.

CHAPTER 10

ENLIGHTENMENT AND GRIEF
(EARLY TO MID-1980s)

D espite the refuge that reading had provided, periods of depression punctuated my years as inevitably as birthdays. Talon-edged emotions could be unleashed at any moment, and I would be crushed by rampaging thoughts instigated by an innocuous conversation, an article in a newspaper, or reports of battles being fought halfway around the world.

In my early twenties, I obsessively read psychoanalytic theory, trying to comprehend why I seemed to be so attached to the noise in my head. Why couldn't I simply let the dark thoughts drift in and out of my mind the way I believed everyone else could? Physical pain was of little consequence; it was my relentless fear that left me bruised.

My closest friend in college was Lisa, who studied sociology; my major was business administration, but my heart was not in it. I had longed to major in English Literature, but my parents had been horrified by the idea. "What would you possibly do with a degree in *English* after graduation?" they wanted to know. "Haven't you noticed that the country is in a recession?" My mother and father were afraid for me. I had never spoken much about marriage as a goal, and they wanted to be certain that I would be self-sufficient. As far back as I can recall, my parents put their children's survival—physical, emotional, financial—at the front of their minds.

Lisa was built with a brain that operated inversely to mine. Any unpleasant thought that dared breach her peace of mind was immediately banished, especially if a quick solution was unavailable. After college, Lisa found a cozy studio apartment in Greenwich Village. Although I still lived with my parents, who had moved to Brooklyn, Lisa's apartment became my de facto home base, and from there she and I explored the downtown punk rock scene. It was also the place to which we retreated when the streets were swallowed by the culture of crack.

When I was with Lisa, I ruminated less and laughed more. With her I felt buoyant and strong enough to exert a counterforce to my self-destructive impulses, and my emotional pain could be sidelined by the thrill of being young in New York City. Lisa's untroubled way of being in the world was contagious, and I felt safe with her. Together, we discovered running, and on my own, I found a therapist and started to unravel my past. Running transformed my physical being. I became calmer, my body toughened with new muscle, my breaths were longer and deeper. My mother, barely into her forties now, became a runner, too, and the three of us ran races together in Central Park.

A fresh wave of feminism had roiled through society in the previous decade, supplanting the earlier mostly home front battles between men and women. A new generation of educated women, bolstered by Ruth Bader Ginsberg's legal successes in dismantling statutory discrimination, had forced monumental social change. Lisa and I marched for the Equal Rights Amendment in Washington DC, and we sat cross-legged on wooden floors in Greenwich Village bookstores, listening enthralled as feminist writers read aloud their theories about patriarchal evils.

Fueled by the electricity of change, I applied for a master's degree in social work, believing that immersing myself in social, academic, and psychological spheres could bring purpose to my life and lasting relief from the battles I fought in my head.

My therapist was a deeply empathic and gentle woman who gave me what seemed like endless space to talk and to dissect my frightening thoughts which were followed by behavior aimed to exorcise those thoughts into non-existence. But I did not know then that by continuing to analyze my pain and obsessive thoughts I was giving fuel to the part of my brain where fear and anxiety reigned. Although I had no way to understand this until much later, I may have inherited a genetic propensity to obsess about the unknown and to live excessively in the fight-or-flight area of my brain. It was not until I was in my fifties that I learned how to reroute my thoughts and finally stare down the reality that I had always run from: the absolute uncertainty of existence.

In 1985, after graduate school, I worked as a medical social worker in New York just as the city was taken hostage by the relentless march of the AIDS virus. From my perch in a large city hospital, I watched as the disease scooped up young men with a hideous fleetness. The AIDS virus shredded ancient layers of immunity that had previously defended against a myriad of microbes—germs that had never caused a lick of trouble to their healthy hosts before the disease. But now, in a matter of weeks, clear-skinned, muscular boys morphed into terrified old men wasted from diarrhea, their skin splotched purple-red from Kaposi's sarcoma. The doctors were left grasping for answers. In private, with each other, they were frantic.

Sometimes I would stand in the doorway or corner of a sickroom and watch mothers who had traveled from their homes in Iowa or Missouri or South Dakota minister to their sons, keeping their boys' feverish faces and hands cool with repeated movements between water basin and hot skin. Mothers often came alone, without the fathers who had been unable to accept their sons' sexuality and now could not bear to watch them die. But the mothers kissed their boys' ravaged bodies and remembered.

Hospitals were deluged with patients so ill they could not walk, eat, or use the toilet by themselves, some so weak they needed oxygen. The hospital's dilemma was that if a patient could be cared for at home, the inpatient stay would not be covered by insurance. This edict threw the finance department into a frenzy. Special nurses were dispatched to gauge the medical legitimacy of hospitalization. Each morning, a pair of utilization review nurses, solid and righteous in their union, marched from one room to the next. Clutching a patient's chart, their heads touching, the nurses whispered grimly to each other as they decided whether discharge was possible.

Usually it was, and since it was my responsibility to plan for the patient's return home, I found these visits terrifying. I'd arrive at the hospital before eight in the morning and rush frantically from one room to another to find at least one of my sixty or so charges trying to ease his newly atrophied legs out of bed. Some were covered in excruciating bed sores; many had been fired from their jobs, had no close family, and lived alone. Running after the informants, I would beg for an extra day or two so I could nail down a complex discharge plan, ensuring the patient would have everything he needed after leaving the safety of the hospital. Some of the patients did have families to return to, and I would talk and plan with them. But focusing on concrete details of after-care was harrowing for the family, and their voices and eyes were dull from fatigue and the effort of trying to keep the reality of their situation from devouring them.

At the end of a particularly punishing day, I would walk to the ice rink in Central Park to skate and allow the icy night wind to clear the clatter from my mind. Moving quickly and gracelessly, falling and getting up again, I would skate for hours in thrall to the stars that lit up the rink so it looked like opalescent glass. I loved the park in winter, especially when it snowed. Everything became quiet then, the sounds of life muffled by the wind and falling snow. Gliding on the ice, I could meld into my surroundings as the world seemed to float, dropping from its usual place on the grid of time and space.

Remembering an early photograph of skaters in Central Park, I could feel the distance between those moments a century and a half before and my own here-and-now melt away, a slippery function of perception. The exhilaration of being fast and alive filled up my chest and pulled me outward into the night, until, sweating, I would stop skating and walk the twenty-five blocks home.

I had loved a young doctor I met at the hospital. In the middle of the day, Peter would come to my hospital floor for a quick hello, maybe a kiss. We became accustomed to the incongruity of being in love in a place of death. Peter had grown up in the Midwest as part of a family of Welsh scientists. He was not Jewish, yet he seemed so familiar. Bookish and refined, he listened to classical music and did not follow sports teams. Peter was kind and earnest, tall and distinguished in his Harris tweed sport coat, a hank of light brown hair falling onto his high forehead. He reminded me of my father; he loved the architecture of Manhattan and how the city's history spoke through its construction. As we roamed the streets together, he showed me the sly crowned salamanders scaling the Petrossian building and explained the physics of a flying buttress while naming the genus of every tree we passed.

But Peter hid from himself and our relationship ended, although neither of us could completely let go. He had pain and secrets he had been numbing with opiates taken from the operating room. Peter died one afternoon at home writing Christmas cards when a poorly calculated injection of morphine stopped his heart. Months before, when he first confessed that he had taken opiates from the operating room, he was anxious and wanted to talk. Sitting stiffly on my plum-colored sofa one night, Peter had become distraught and cradled his head in his hands. "I did it once a couple of years ago. A relationship had just ended and I was sad and stressed from work. And I'd just started weekends in the ER."

I was shocked and scared by Peter's admission; the perfect man was devolving in front of me. Probing reluctantly, I convinced him to see a therapist and then I let it go. It was as if I were following some imagined rule of non-Jewishness: do not intrude. I did not encourage Peter to explore his emotions as I often did with my friends. Eager to be done with this threat to our relationship, I asked only for his promise that it would never happen again. I needed to know that it was a one-off, prompted by pressure at work. With blinders firmly in place, I had closed myself off to anything else he needed to bring to me. I wanted Peter to be strong for me, because when we were together I felt encircled and protected by his non-Jewish pedigree.

A career in social work had made sense because I wanted to help people. I had always intervened when I saw bullies in action; abusive behavior enraged me. Since childhood, I would not mind my own business if someone was being harassed or victimized. While intuitively it seems logical that such a need could result from having grown up with the greatest mass victimization in history as my primary frame of reference, I never felt this intense fury when I was the person being hurt.

So why didn't I feel compelled to save Peter? The prospect of destroying his own career, of betraying all his years of study and clinical practice, must have petrified him. Yet, like an officious schoolmarm, I instructed him to stop lifting morphine. My gut instinct, far more compelling than any rational thinking, was that his drug use would weaken his ability to protect me. I do not believe that my need to help people was completely altruistic; instead, it may also have served the purpose of ensuring my own safety. People liked and appreciated and cared for me when I was listening to them, searching for solutions to their dilemmas.

I could have felt, unconsciously, that if I engaged deeply enough with people, if the connection was strong enough, even the Nazis would care for me and protect me. My adult mind can see how unreasonable such a conclusion is, but my more primitive and egocentric child's mind was driven to make the world feel safe. Because hadn't the Jewish children of Europe been deemed unnecessary liabilities and disposed of?

CHAPTER 11

COURTSHIP
(LATE 1980s)

Having lost the courage to continue watching young men disappear, I left the hospital after a year. Now I was thirty-three and had begun to dream of babies. Suddenly, I saw them everywhere, and their scent infiltrated my thoughts and saturated me until I was perfectly marinated with both the hormones and the will I would need to marry Brian.

I had never seriously pondered a reality of marriage and children. My friends and I were feminists; we did not consciously think about those things. But then the hardwiring kicked in and there it was, a palpable pull, an internal disarray that could only be made right with a child.

I met Brian at my next job on the Lower East Side of Manhattan counseling teenagers who were at risk of dropping out of school. I was working at night on a post-graduate degree in clinical social work—the credential I needed to become a proper psychotherapist. My new job brought relatively little stress and left me with enough free time and emotional energy to study.

I knew that a life with Brian would not be gentle. He had given me fair notice of what was to come. Not only did I ignore the warning, but I also seemed to gravitate toward what it foretold; I probably searched it out. I always pushed away the gentle boys who tried to woo me. With them, nothing more than a brotherly connection was possible. They were kind and Jewish, but it was as if their sameness made attraction impossible.

I did not agree with many of Brian's values and attitudes, and this attraction was unlike any I had known before. I *needed* to know Brian, and I *needed* him to like me. He was like a bright thing glowing wildly next to a gray landscape. I had to grab hold of this beautiful thing. I was not curious about what I felt; I just knew I wanted him. But had I thought more analytically, I might have dissuaded myself from marrying him, and that was the last thing I desired.

How deep must the crevices of the brain be to hold the sort of ancient information that can incite such longing? I imagine that somewhere in the memory deposits section of my brain, a cell latched onto Brian's sparkling image and sent out an urgent call to action to a neurotransmitter floating in a synapse, which began then to swim furiously to reach a receptor cell. The neurotransmitter's mission: to deliver instructions to win Brian, a brilliantly eligible non-Jew who would keep me tucked safely under his navy-blue–blazered wing, along with a possible membership to the local anti-Semitic country club.

Working as a psychologist with the same children I counseled, Brian seemed reserved and at times aloof. I saw that he did not connect well with the kids who were predominantly Black and Latino, nor with the left-leaning social workers whom he was charged with supervising. Dark and serious, Brian exuded privilege. He was exotic to me, a rare creature. There was an elegance to the way he dressed, the way he held himself and arranged his limbs, that immediately evoked movies I had watched after school, where everyone sashayed around opulent drawing rooms in velvet dressing gowns and had cocktails before dinner.

Brian was working on a postdoctoral degree in psychoanalysis when we met, and I was going to New York University at night. He was articulate, and the way he spoke was enticing. I wanted to know everything he knew about the mind. But his knowledge came with weighty opinions that I struggled to distill, and I wasn't sure about the depth of his character. I rarely disagreed with him, but I did one time when he opined that most people were psychotic. He made this pronouncement during a walk on Broadway after we had watched a nihilistic movie that concluded with the end of humanity.

"How can you say such a thing, Brian?" I was incredulous.

"It's a fact."

The thundering overreach of it and what it said about him and his experience in the world shocked me. I saw disaffection in him, an almost listless disinterest in the children we worked with. He could neither pronounce nor remember some of their names but didn't seem to notice or care. I was embarrassed for him.

He was from Connecticut, the northwestern part of the state where the landscape quickly turned rural as one traveled north, and incomes and satisfaction levels were high. Full of lovely white churches with tall steeples, country clubs and lots of snow, the setting intoxicated me. The novels of my youth, with white Christmases and majestic lawns surrounding stately but welcoming homes, had come to life, and I could not have felt more delighted.

Married once before for less than a year, Brian used a psychoanalytic term to describe his ex-wife to me. He explained that she was an "as if" type of personality. This meant that she only behaved as if she were a healthy person. I saw her once at an evening social event for Brian's postdoctoral program where all the psychoanalysts and students danced frenetically, apparently thrilled to let loose and exhibit what was libidinous and normally kept under wraps. Brian's former wife seemed pretty and sweet, and I watched her closely, looking for interactions that showed she was acting "as if."

As I look back, Brian did not hide any aspects of his character from me. His aloofness signified an impermeability to injury, the other side of a coin I was all too familiar with. Brian's cool detachment was a more palatable dish than the stifling embrace of my family with its compulsive over protecting, over loving, and over feeding. He seemed to inhabit a world dominated by the ethos of those who knew no fear, and I needed to belong to them, not to my own. To be a member of this insular "Gentlemen's Agreement" crowd—a synthesis of everything that had been written in the books of my childhood and vividly illustrated in my mind—was the antithesis of the Holocaust. I craved this world of utopian America, yet it was an unrelenting reminder of how far from belonging I was.

As a child, I thought that surrounding myself with superficial beauty could keep tragedy at bay. To escape the acid taste of nonbelonging, I retreated to the idealized worlds that were described in my books and portrayed on television. In that paradise, families kept their cool, and the tantrums of the teenagers on *Leave It to Beaver* and the *Donna Reed Show* were quickly contained and resolved in the embrace of parents who understood and explained and soothed. Afterward, everyone would sit down for dinner at the beautifully laid dining table on which platters of fried chicken, biscuits, and tureens of lump-free mashed potatoes were artistically set with nary a potato latke in sight. Concealed within these tableaux were existences that I later discovered were neither perfect nor untroubled.

Brian liked me; things moved quickly and I allowed myself to be moved by him. I thought that with time he would begin to smile spontaneously, and that if I persevered, I could open him up, and his capacity for love and kindness would be revealed.

On my first trip to Bethel, Brian's hometown, we were headed to the wedding of his close friend from school, Neal, who was marrying again after a brief first marriage. The drive felt other-worldly, snow falling steadily for the second part of the trip as we made our way north and then headed west. The flakes, plump and lazy, danced in the car's high beams before hitting the ground. Turning off the highway, we drove into town on dark secondary roads, great slumbering arteries that sliced through corn and wheat fields and acres of forest. Roads that could be mistaken one for another in the dark.

The small white church was set back from the main street behind tall hedges. Its white steeple stretched high and then evanesced into the darkness. Inside, the church was surprisingly spacious. Guests sat in the wooden pews and clapped as the couple made vows to each other and were married. It was a beautiful and simple wedding. The newlyweds were shy and gracious as the guests ate from sparsely laid-out platters of wedding cake and drank champagne from plastic flutes.

I wondered when the food would be served, but Brian said that it was a low-key affair, just champagne and wedding cake. It was not like every other wedding I had been to, where guest after guest elbowed each other at the massive buffet to get to the shrimp first. We congratulated Neal and his pretty, freckled bride, Cathy. The elated groom whispered to Brian, "I see you have found your Cathy!"

The quiet elegance of Brian's mother's home was frayed; his parents had divorced years before. The table manners were a marvel; nobody spoke with mouths full of food. Nobody called in Yiddish from one end of the table to the other, "Darling! Eat some kishkes! Eat, ess, ess, my darling!"

I was entranced by his family. If they were a little reserved toward me, it would only be until they knew I was there to stay. The first time I spent the night in his mother's home, I slept in the second-floor guest room of the white colonial house, which was set back on a double corner lot. The house was large to my eyes and shaped like an L. The guest room overlooked the front yard, and three windows were dressed in pink nylon tulle with floppy bows that resembled rabbit ears. The ruffled edges crisscrossed and tied at the window sash.

The night looked in, framed by trees stripped clean, their longer branches rapping on the glass in time with the wind. We were "in the country," and the silence was heavy. I heard the rustling sounds of small animals foraging, their furred contours blurring into the night as they hid their loot.

Brian slept down the hall in his childhood bedroom. I hoped that he'd had his fill of beer and would sleep deeply and forget about his plan to visit me later. I wanted to sleep undisturbed, breathing in the delicious icy air coming from the window I had opened. This was a true American home, and as I admired the green-and-pink flowered walls, I felt the warm caress of privilege settle over me under the heat of the blankets.

It was the difference that I fell in love with, and I thought that I would never feel suffocated in this place with these people. It was only a small problem that many of the town's residents, not having grown up with Jews or knowing more than a few in their lives, did not particularly want to know them.

In grade school, I had been on the receiving end of the more forthright sort of anti-Semitism, the "you killed Christ," "dirty Jew," or "kike" type. This sort was more genteel, subtle, but no less apparent. At times, there was also an assumption that the Jewish outsider's mental thickness and lack of sophistication impaired any ability to ascertain condescension. For example, Brian's father, hoping to make me feel included, would look meaningfully at me from the corner of his eye as he would describe his colleague, Mr. Goldberg, who had been an occasional guest in their home.

"Mr. Goldberg was—" and here Brian's father would pause while giving me a meaningful sidewise glance, "shrewd, very shrewd, a real businessman!"

CHAPTER 12

THE MAN I MARRIED
(1990)

The first time I witnessed the ugly side of Brian's character, I was driving onto the Cross Island Parkway, a major, bloated artery. Having grown up in New York City with plenty of public transportation, I had never learned to drive, and Brian felt that this would not be helpful in creating the life for us that he thought we should have. So, at the age of thirty-four, I took driving lessons.

I had stopped the car at the end of the narrow ramp, waiting for an opportunity to merge onto the highway that resembled a runaway river. I was afraid to move; my body simply had not had enough driving experience to earn my trust. I was not sure that the movements ordered by my brain to my foot would result in exactly the right amount of pressure to the pedals: strong enough but also gentle, so as not to cause the deaths of a dozen people, their wrecked cars waiting like trash to be cleared from the road's shoulder.

After a few minutes of enduring my hesitation, Brian became agitated. "Go!" he yelled. His face contorted and turned red. I could see the pores of his skin. In that moment, it seemed that his head floated off his neck and positioned itself in front of me, blocking my view of the road. "You are so passive-aggressive!" he yelled.

I had been scared, and now I was also confused. Passive-aggressive? What could he mean? I told myself to look left, to be brave, to turn my head to face the rush of cars. A slight gap in the churning river appeared. I turned the wheel hard, too fast, and the car lunged. *Turn it back slowly,* I instructed myself. *Keep going. Now, straighten it out. Yes, done. Breathe.*

That night Brian sobbed noisily and begged to be forgiven. I told him I was leaving; it was the first time.

"Never again, never again, I will never treat you like that again! I don't know what came over me," he said. "Please, we are supposed to be together!"

And that was how my complicity started, a partnering with this man. In that moment, I began the decade-long process of shielding myself and later my children from the fallout of an ugliness that I could not fix, an ugliness I believed I had provoked. But this was the naiveté of my younger self; it is rare to succeed in changing another human being. One transforms because of the value that such change brings to oneself. If Brian had felt that he could not lose me, then change might have followed.

I failed to fix him, and the hurt of it became less and less painful over the years. My mind had used its power of denial, observing all from a distance, yet with a breadth that was never far enough away. I still have trouble comprehending it, but the shame and guilt for living was continuing to orchestrate my choices and behaviors. It was as if my guilt could only be assuaged by my grief.

A paradox had grown from the competition between my unconscious motivations and what I rationally knew to be true. I sought out a marriage that I knew would fail. I reached for it because only in such a union could I and my future children be safe, hidden in the plain sight of Brian's non-Jewish tribe. It was the club of white Anglo-Saxon America where my Jewish race would be forgiven and I would be protected. And when reality diverged from my fantasies, I did not listen. Once during an argument over his disapproval of my therapist, Brian called me a "Dirty Jew." How quickly I swept that statement away, hiding it deep in my consciousness where it would be out of reach.

Years later, when I could allow my delusions to surface and show themselves, I understood that it would be from Brian that I needed protection.

That spring, we took our first vacation together to Colorado to ski; I was excited. Brian taught me to ski, and I loved flying down the hills, often rolling to the bottom. The second night, Brian became angry at me for checking in with my friend and colleague Denise at the school where we all worked. I was worried about a boy whom I was counseling. He was too big for his britches but small and tender and had a way of getting himself bullied. I had asked Denise how he was doing. Brian screamed at me while I made the call.

I watched as the soda bottle that he flung—toward the kitchen or toward me—arced gracefully before hitting the wall. Clutching the phone tight against my face to muffle the sounds, I shut down my reaction. But the sensation of choking, working to get the words out while struggling to breathe, would soon become familiar. Brian had thrown something, and I had to make what he did go away. Afterward, when he was calm, he promised me that this was an aberration, that it was only his frustration at my willingness to take something from our time together that had caused this eruption. In this way, I learned another thing that I must not do to provoke him.

Early the next morning, we rode to the top of the mountain on the chair lift, and on the way up passed signs with black diamonds painted on them. I was a novice skier, but I knew what the signs meant. I told Brian that I could not go down those hills.

I said, "I'm just not comfortable, and the snow here is so soft—like there is nothing under my skis. I can find an easier slope and meet you at the bottom."

Brian stared at me without expression. "Fuck you," he said suddenly and, whipping his skis around, flew down the mountain.

I felt shame engulf me as my blood heated beneath the insulation of my ski clothes. I was a pariah; Brian would only speak like this to me because I deserved it. But I hated him and hated myself for being with him. I could almost feel the dichotomy physically splitting me. It was not an unforgivable act that Brian had committed, yet it was unexpected, and the speed in which it happened was cruel and piercing because I had not been prepared. This casual callousness, I knew, augured future hurt.

I stood still in that spot for a few minutes and worked to lift my legs, which were now knee-deep and unmanageable in the soft snow. I looked around for signs that would point to an easier way down. It was early still, and that part of the massive mountain was empty and, in its silence, glorious. The trails of new snow were corrugated with bumps, and tall pines marked the no-go areas. The air was visible, pristine tufts of icy vapor. The contrast between the beauty of the scene and the nauseating humiliation coursing through me seemed depraved. I found my way down the mountain, and this time neither one of us spoke about what had happened.

That evening, we had dinner with an old friend and her husband who were vacationing, coincidentally, at the same resort. They were curious about us, our relationship, and somehow, perhaps noticing our reticence with each other, spoke about their own rough times as a couple. They told us that once a year, one of them would pack the car and leave for a day or two with their children, and that marriages could be turbulent.

I equated their experiences with what had already begun to foul our relationship and was comforted by the idea that maybe Brian and I were a normal new couple trying to adjust to each other and that over time we would find our fit. Despite reassurances to myself, I could see what lay ahead for us. But I was driven to complete the process, and we became engaged on the flight back to New York.

My parents reacted solemnly to the news as we shared a champagne toast. I remember Brian looking like the proverbial cat after a tasty avian lunch and my sad parents sitting so straight-backed and awkward at the edge of the sofa in Brian's apartment. I wanted it all to be wonderful—it was my engagement! But my mother's face was an accusing mirror reflecting what I already knew.

There had been an instant antipathy between my mother and Brian. She thought him arrogant, and Brian thought her judgmental. Perhaps I needed to have friction with my parents to feel separate, capable of an independent act, especially one that was going to allow me to be part of Brian's world. We decided to marry in Bethel where he had grown up. We brought my parents with us to look for a nonreligious wedding venue that would make both our families comfortable and ended up deciding on an inn built in the eighteenth century. I needn't have worried about offending Brian's family. I had run as fast as I could to a small Connecticut town where Jews were so scarce that it had no synagogue.

My mother did not speak directly to me about her feelings, but they were clear. She was late to our wedding, and along with my aunt and grandmother, whom she had enlisted as allies, arrived in Connecticut just moments before the wedding service began. My father, in his confrontation-averse affability, had come alone the day before to join the men in their pre-wedding golf games at the country club, although he did not know how to play the game.

CHAPTER 13

A BABY ARRIVES
(1991)

I was two weeks overdue, and my obstetrician, Dr. Moreno, an intensely focused, impossibly handsome man, wanted to take the baby out. He decided to induce labor that night.

Earlier that day, Brian and I had eaten lunch at a restaurant known for its original 1940s décor. Swivel bar stools stood at attention at the counter, and the owners, two brothers who had inherited the luncheonette, wore white cotton jackets and made egg creams and hamburgers for patrons eager to show their children part of their own youth. I ate an egg salad sandwich, hesitating for a moment as I considered the possibility of vomiting during labor.

Noah was stubborn and did not want to come out. Hooked up to a heart monitor, I was instructed to lie still and lean on my right elbow for an accurate reading. The maternity floor was buzzing; a major sports star had just announced that he was HIV-positive. Brian sat on the window seat in the labor room and read the newspaper. He chatted with the doctor about the spectacular headline. I wished he would sit next to me.

The labor was long, and morning had come. Forceps were not working, and I was relieved when they were put aside. I had been afraid that the doctor would accidentally pull Noah's head off using the striated rubber suction cap of the forceps, which looked like a medieval instrument of torture. I was wheeled into a bright operating room where wires were attached to my chest. People came in and out of the room. The monitor showed that Noah's heartbeat was becoming erratic, and the doctor did not like that.

Someone said, "We're prepping you for a C-section, just in case."

I looked for Dr. Moreno. He stood to my left, next to my leg. I had been pushing for two hours and the epidural was no longer working. I felt that what had been whole inside of me was now in tatters, a torn-apart mess of bone and flesh. I cannot recall where Brian was during the worst of the labor. I remember him being distressed as he walked alongside me when I was taken to the operating room.

"It hurts too much," I said, speaking to Dr. Moreno's eyes, black over his mask. "I can't push anymore. Please just give me more of the epidural." But I had already made the same request back in the labor room, where the answer had been no.

"It's too late now, Rena. Come on, just give me one really good, *strong* push."

I thought I might pass out at his words, but the nurses were saying Noah was too far down, and the C-section could be problematic. It felt as if my lower half had been blown to bits and I was being told to expel what was still intact inside of me. I pulled myself up onto my elbows and looked at Dr. Moreno. He was the only one I saw in that room with its glaring lights. My mind moved from the operating room to his office.

Months earlier we had spoken about the genocide in Bosnia, and he had told me that at any given moment there were a hundred wars going on throughout the world. Dr. Moreno said this in such a defeated tone that he was embarrassed and apologized at the following check-up. Conversations with him had felt like I was reentering the world and hinted that life was long and its course could be changed.

"Push, now! Hard!" he said. I knew I could not push with hesitation. Noah would stay stuck if I were tentative. I must embrace the act and the pain that would come with it. It was an impossible concept, but I knew if I wanted to make it out of the hospital alive with my baby, I would have to accept the pain. I pushed again and burned inside.

Dr. Moreno, relieved, called out that he saw the head. "Now, one more push!"

I obeyed, and Noah flew out covered in something white and chalky.

The doctor caught Noah and held out a pair of scissors to Brian. Holding the umbilical cord between his fingers, Dr. Moreno marked a spot and said, "Cut."

Brian looked at him.

The doctor pushed the scissors into Brian's hand. "Cut it!"

Brian cut the cord, and I was done. Bliss.

The next few days were marked by pain and delight in Noah's birth. He was born jaundiced, and the hospital had sent me home—utilization review nurses apparently also walked the halls of maternity wards—but wanted to keep Noah under observation until his color normalized. Worrying that he would be bottle-fed a mixture of sugar and water by an over-eager or tired nurse, I took the subway downtown to nurse him. I was excited to see Noah after the night's absence. The subway was crowded, and the vibrations of the train resonated unpleasantly in my humbled body. I had an all-over sensation of rawness, as if there were hundreds of live wires scattered inside of me, but soon Noah was in my arms again, and I was filled with my baby. Tucked into a rocking chair in the neonatal ward, I felt the riot in my body settle as I nursed him.

Two days later, Noah was home. Brian had left the apartment early for work. The day stretched on, and I started to feel as if I were spinning, again from the inside. I did not recognize these sensations for the hormone fluctuations they probably were. I tried to reach Brian by phone, but he was not returning my messages. I fed Noah well, and he slept sweetly and hardly cried. But my body felt raw, old, and tired. I needed to talk to someone. Later in the evening when Brian finally came home, I was relieved but frightened. Feeling spent, I began to cry.

"I can't do this, Brian. I am so scared! I don't know how to be a mother. How can I possibly be a good mother if I don't know how?" I had gotten up from the couch where I had been resting. I held out my hands, imploring him to comfort me. I remember him standing very still, at the dining table, watching me with an unfocused stare as if he were looking right through me. Then I became hysterical. I wanted him to collect me in his arms like a package that had come loose from its wrappings. And to tell me that I could do it, that of course I would be a good mother.

In a frenzy of desperation for reassurance and kindness, I pushed and pushed for anything from him. A gesture of love, of comprehension. But he gave me nothing, just silence, and I continued to weep and remonstrate.

My vision a fog of tears, I moved unsteadily toward the bathroom to try to calm myself. Silently Brian followed me, and I felt him push me on the back, and I sank to the cold floor. He pummeled me with his fists and kicked me low on my back as I lay with my eyes open on the bathroom floor, the tiny hexagonal tiles of white porcelain staring back at me. I watched the barrage as if from above. He screamed at me, cursed my existence. My arms circled the base of the toilet and held it tight as his feet and fists came down on me. I held it as I had wanted to be held.

Then suddenly it was over.

Brian walked out of the bathroom, and my first thoughts were of Noah, but he still slept. Then of the neighbors; there had been cries and screaming. Could they have called the police? If someone had, would they take Noah?

Nauseous and wretched with fear, I let myself be soothed by Brian, who had composed himself. Speaking softly, he held me as he explained what had happened. It was, he said, the logical consequence of my hysteria and insecurities, which reminded him of his mother's inadequacies and neuroticism. It had been too much for him to bear, Brian said. He felt helpless and vulnerable the way he had as a child, and of course he, too, had been under enormous stress since Noah's birth.

I accepted the explanation that my uncontrolled emotion was responsible for Brian's reaction. Depleted afterward, I was certain, as I had been before, that my own defects had caused this to happen.

When Brian agreed to meet with my therapist, Willa, to "process" the incident, I was hopeful. But at the meeting, Brian was no longer contrite. Believing that he had been unfairly provoked, set up even, he rose from his chair abruptly and stormed out of her office midway through the session.

"I don't have to listen to this!" he yelled. His face contorted in anger and his hands clenched into fists as he strode out of the room.

When I looked at Willa's face, frozen and uncomprehending, I felt the loathsome pathogens spread through me, rooting. The only way out, the only way to make things right, was for me to be the one culpable.

Connection with Brian, the kind I craved, eluded me, but in its place, a bond emerged each time he became violent. In the beginning when it happened, we cried and clung together, and he made promises. There was a terrible symmetry to these episodes. Frustration and anger hovered always, even as we tried to talk about it. I worked to push away the knowledge that violence could never be a normal part of any relationship. Sometimes I succeeded in rationalizing that my behavior and my character were so inflammatory that any man would have reacted the way Brian had.

My tyrannical need to bring every submerged emotion out into the open had been honed in childhood, when I tried to pull from my mother anything she could be hiding from me. What had been a normal mechanism to protect children during the war, what my mother had learned from her mother, was anathema to me. I was often suspicious of words, suspecting that the truth lay in what had *not* been said, in what had been concealed. With Brian, I might say or do something to pry open the gates of fragile equilibrium that existed, and then he would erupt. When it was over, I was always ashamed, and I think that the shame was a way of keeping alive the belief in my own culpability, because if I felt shame, then it was my fault, and if so, how could I leave? Believing that I had pushed Brian to this aberrant place, I felt closer to this man who beat me with his fists, as if with the pouring out of his rage, I had eased his pain and finally gained access to his heart.

CHAPTER 14

TRANSITIONS
(EARLY 1990s)

After I married Brian, the defenses that had shielded me from what I saw at work became porous. I had trouble staying neutral or maintaining even a minimal distance from the pain and disarray I witnessed.

Funding for social programs had decreased and my caseload had ballooned. I was tired. Social work had consumed me, and I ached for the children, who were, by necessity, heartbreakingly independent. Many of them had parents who had been drained by life's battles and rendered too impotent to guide their children through the barbed wire of adolescence in New York City. The students were infectiously honest, sometimes to the point of causing embarrassment when their candor was directed toward me. Their identities, just starting to bloom, leaned heavily on self-expression. They wore baseball caps adorned with their graphic art, pins, and symbols.

During one of my lunchtime walks, I stumbled into the showroom of a fabric company that designed blooming prints as colorful as jewels. I wondered if women would wear pretty baseball caps to protect their faces from the sun.

My mother had always been vigilant about her skin. She would admonish me to stay away from it, to run from the sun.

"Rena," she would say, "put a hat on, or you'll be a prune in no time!"

The kind Danish saleswoman, Kirsten, gave me a stack of twelve-inch square fabric samples, each one large enough to make one baseball cap. After researching in a New Jersey telephone book, I found a family-run hat manufacturer who agreed to sew my sample caps. An older man named Seymour and his nephew Dennis ran the factory. Dennis listened to my vision and asked his most talented employee, Joan, who normally stitched McDonald's and Kentucky Fried Chicken caps, to sew my samples. Dennis patiently heard out my plan in his dusty office. His uncle Seymour stuck his head in through the doorway. Speaking loudly to be heard above the sound of sewing machines, Seymour said, "Hey, Dennis, you got a long enough piece of paper for her order?"

It took me a few seconds to get the joke, and its effect was to make me immediately feel at home.

Two weeks later, armed with a hatbox full of bright floral-patterned baseball caps, I received an order from a pretty Connecticut boutique where the owner and her assistants gleefully pulled the caps out of the hatbox with the eagerness of children at a candy counter. My second order was from New York's most elegant department store; I had sneaked up to the ninth-floor hat buyer's office and poked my head into the small room.

After recovering from her shock that I had gotten past the layers of security consisting of one receptionist reading a fashion magazine, the buyer handed me a small piece of construction paper on which she had taped wool yarn in plum, blue, red, rust, and brown.

"These are our fall colors," she said. "Use this palette as a guide, and make me two dozen different caps. If they sell, we will do lot of business together. If they don't, you'll never hear from us again."

Baseball caps in silk jacquard, herringbone wool tweed, and Scottish wool plaid, all lined in contrasting colors and patterns, tumbled from Joan's sewing machine. I delivered the hats, and the fashion stylist put them on mannequins in the window. They sold out, and the hat buyer and I did a lot of business together. I sold to other stores, showing my hats to whoever was in charge. Soon other department stores and catalogs bought them, and a TV shopping channel followed.

I named the company Samcaps after my cat, Sam. I was the president and Brian the vice president. After a year of trying to do both jobs, I left social work. Customers began to ask for beach clothes to coordinate with the hats, so I sourced new factories that sewed clothes, and Samcaps grew. The days were exhilarating, and I had trouble falling asleep at night because I was so eager to start each day. It was as if I had recovered the part of me that was shut down when I ran away from art school.

Brian worked with me sometimes, though we had different perspectives about money and how the business should be spending it. He wanted to expand—too quickly, I thought. I wanted to wait until the company grew before increasing our expenses. I was always worried about cash flow. Our second son, Cal, was born a year and a half after Noah, and we rented a larger apartment near the southern entrance of Central Park. The sleek building felt too elegant for us, and the rent was high. Brian had been working a few jobs as a consulting psychologist while trying to build a private practice but had difficulty making a go of it. Money was a constant worry, and we paid for private health insurance ourselves, an unsustainable cost. Brian said that we ought to leave New York because we would never earn enough money to live the way we should.

After a few months of sending out his résumé, Brian found a position as a school psychologist in an economically depressed eighteenth-century Connecticut mill town which had risen where two rivers met. The town, once a hub of manufacturing, was gray and littered with abandoned factories. It seemed indifferent to its own neglect.

The school system, like the town, sat at the bottom of the state's rankings. Brian had often expressed his opinion that a school counselor was as low as a psychologist could go professionally. And the school he landed in kept that belief present in his mind as an insult delivered all day long. The pay was low, a constant humiliation, but the health insurance was good, and we decided to make the move. Believing that Connecticut promised the best life for our family, we left New York when Cal was three months old.

CHAPTER 15

RON

I believe I saw Ron on the day we left New York. It was late August 1993, and we were headed to our new life in Connecticut. Hoping to seize twenty-four hours of vacation in Maine, we spent a night in a Kennebunkport hotel overlooking the steel-gray waters of the North Atlantic. Noah was nearly two years old and Cal an infant of three months.

Although I had not planned to stop nursing Cal so soon, I weaned him that day. I'd hoped for a few more months, but Cal was colicky and screamed every afternoon between four and seven o'clock. The colic was brutal. Cal's tiny red face told a story of pain that I could not fix. After he was finally soothed, he would sleep and then would wake to eat. Often, in those first months as the systems of his body adjusted to life outside of me, Cal would vomit immediately after he fed. Then I would bathe him, change his nightgown and the sheets of his crib, and feed him once more. Sometimes he vomited twice in one night, and I ran out of clean sheets and had to improvise. Propped up in bed, I nursed him until we both fell asleep. I felt guilty over this passive breastfeeding, afraid that I would roll over in my sleep and crush him.

So I weaned him too soon, and I regretted the impulsive act almost immediately. I felt the foolishness of what I had done as a bitter ache in my bones. Was I looking for peace, an even cadence to my life? I had long known that there would be no peace while I was married to this man who offered up such elegant and compelling explanations for his violence. Could I have thought that this one act of physical independence from my child might change the ugly syntax and mercilessness of my interactions with my husband?

Feeding my babies at night was difficult because I felt a profound loneliness, a sense of complete isolation that was physically painful. Alone in the deep night when nothing, not even my reflection in the mirror, seemed familiar, I felt that my usefulness, at least from an evolutionary perspective, had ended. Thoughts that were counter to everything I knew I should be thinking moved into my head.

I was terrified for my children's mortality and my own and could not imagine a world where they did not exist, where I was not there to care for them when they grew old. The idea that they might leave the world without having me with them haunted me. The stories I'd heard of blissful motherhood with its promises of joyful bonding and supreme connection seemed like fairy tales spun in the service of a higher maternal order.

And there on the living room sofa looking at the tops of their busy heads, I grieved, feeling that my children and I were nothing more than cogs in the uncaring wheel of human existence. The thoughts infected me and despair settled in. Had I talked about this to someone, I might have understood that sadness after birth was not unusual, and its grip would likely loosen with the calming of my pregnancy hormones. But then, without the distraction of self-recrimination, I might have had to face being mother alongside Brian as father.

At the hotel, Cal and I were alone together at a round table large enough for six in the cavernous, old-fashioned dining room with the verandah that had a view of the water. Brian was walking with Noah along the grounds of the once-grand hotel that seemed to grow out of the cliffs lining that part of the jagged northern Maine coast. Gardens surrounded the place, and uneven stone steps led down to the road where one could cross and arrive at the beach, which was cold and uncultivated, a bleak echo of the cliffs.

Two men sat at a neighboring table, just the two of them. Good friends, I thought then. Brothers, I learned years later. In his thirties, the younger man was dark, with eyes that seemed almost black. His nose was prominent and the bones of his face were set high so that he looked in part to be Native American. The man's eyes drifted around the room lazily. He was very lean with long legs and arms, and I felt chagrin at my own body, softer and messier since Cal was born.

The men were chatting quietly, the plates in front of them empty. I was conscious of Cal's discomfort. He needed to burp, and I was afraid he would spit up on my shoulder. Embarrassed, I hoped the men would leave so I could take care of him.

Soon, they rose from the table. Reluctantly, it seemed, as if this lunch was the last meal of the final day of a wonderful trip. When the younger man walked behind my chair, I felt the air displace, and my breathing slowed. As he moved, I turned, and he leaned his body in slightly. He looked at me and smiled. I was stunned. Years later, Ron said that he had fallen in love with me in that instant.

Gathering Cal and my things, I went to our room at the end of the long, windowed corridor lined with antique chests and fragile-looking chairs on narrow, curved legs. The room was decorated with tiny print wallpaper and the furniture gleamed, the wood worn and beautiful. I settled against the pillows of the bed and nursed Cal there for the last time. He slept afterward, folding himself onto me, sinking into my new-mother's softness. I heard the key turn, and Brian walked into the room with Noah. He did not look at us as he strode quickly across the room.

"Are you ready?" he said. "Can we get going? I'm getting bored now. This place is so retro old money. Really preten-tious." He sounded mildly disgusted but also envious. I picked up Noah.

"Mama," he said.

"Did he have something to eat?" I asked Brian.

"He didn't seem hungry."

Brian walked into the bathroom and I moved from the bed and changed Noah's heavy diaper. Once again, I was surprised at the serious expression in his eyes. Noah was an inquisitive toddler. In his face, I could see infancy disappearing. It had already given way to an awareness emanating from his brown eyes, which always made me think of a lake with no bottom. One day a woman would be enthralled with those eyes, heed nothing but her love, and leap headfirst into that lake.

"Did you have fun, sweetheart?"

"Pity flowers, Mama."

"Pretty flowers? Where, sweetheart?"

"Outside, Mama." He turned to look at his brother. "Cal crying," he said, his butterfly-wing brows knitting together.

"His tummy hurts," I told Noah, moving back to the bed to pick up Cal, who was now awake and had begun to thrash from the pain that had plagued us all. "He'll feel better soon."

Later that evening, we sat at a long wooden table in a restaurant called The Lobster Shack that had red-and-white checkered placemats featuring cheerful lobsters with snap-ping claws. No surprise there. On the way to dinner, driving along the dark coastal road, Brian had pointed out the home of George Bush. "Man, they are so rich," he said, with envy of wealth animating his voice like caffeine.

It was dusk and the salty, wet air was heavy. I looked at the spreading compound Brian had pointed to. In the dark, the main house seemed to hang over the rocky edge of the jutting coast like a misshapen appendage about to fall. In the water below, small dinghies were tied loosely to the dock and wobbled in the shallows, the occasional beam from a nearby lighthouse releasing everything from darkness. *Was there peace in this family?* I wondered. I always wanted to know what lay underneath, unseen.

At the restaurant, Cal pulled at my dress. I took out the bottle that I had mixed in the hotel bathroom and moved in. Cal pushed his lips together ferociously, his face collapsing in on itself. Shaking his head from side to side, he started to scream. The diners looked up and around for the offending baby. Brian turned his head and looked at me, joining in the silent accusation. The sensation of being on the outside, alone at the edge of the world, was as old as my memory's reach.

Brian said, "You really need to take him outside. It's rude. We'll switch in a little while." He returned to his meal.

I looked at my dinner plate and stood up. I walked the length of the parking lot with Cal in my arms. He had stopped crying and his fingers were weaving into my neck. His creamy skin shone as if lit from inside and his rounded form stamped a glorious silhouette against the night. Cal smiled flirtatiously and grabbed at my hair with his tiny fists. His body felt like warm dough, and I was drunk on his smile.

This marriage will die a slow death, I thought.

CHAPTER 16

TWO CHILDREN
OF THE HOLOCAUST

Years later, Ron and I often debated whether that encounter at the hotel in Kennebunkport had in fact taken place.

"It wasn't you and it wasn't me," I would say.

"Yes, it was, I'd bet my life on it," he would respond without fail. "I remember how harried you looked, the baby spitting up on you. But you were so beautiful." What Ron did not say until years later was that in the seconds of our wordless exchange, he was already plotting a life with me. The image exploded in his head like a display of fireworks and was just as quickly dismissed as the greatest of impossibilities.

Looking at me, Ron thought my happiness was a given, and my position, as mother and certainly wife, fixed. His offhand comment to his brother was, "Did you see that woman?" But his thought was that there was nothing more absurd than himself and this woman *and* the baby together. He took in the picture of Cal in my arms, drooling on one shoulder, a towel draped over the other. It wasn't a pretty sight, he later said, but never had he so longed for a woman. Handsome and silver-tongued, with tried-and-true abilities of seduction, Ron could not imagine a way in, and it drove him crazy.

His confessions embarrassed me; my own thoughts had been far less articulate. But what I did remember was that during the moment when he looked at me, I was filled with all the possibilities of the world, and everything that was sour in my life condensed to a single fat crystal and floated away.

Ron and I had been born in the middle of the last century a year apart, a decade after the war that conceived and marked us. He grew up in Mississippi in a small house on a new street in Gulfport, close enough to the warm gulf waters to swim whenever he wanted. I was raised in a flat part of Queens where brick Cape Cod houses cut the monotony of the rows of low-slung, horseshoe-shaped buildings referred to as "courts" by the people who lived in them. There, the children played in the grassy ovals formed by the buildings' flanks and were guarded by chain link fencing.

In childhood, we were both deeply attached to our fears. Just as the aftermath of the Holocaust lived inside of me, Ron's consciousness of World War II was delivered to him by his father, Zeke, who had served in Europe. Zeke's memories of the slaughter tormented him, and he was a wounded, complex man. Frequent collisions with his family came with these wounds, a toll paid by his wife and children.

Ron was the sort of child who wrote dark poetry about the aggressions of his father. And I was the sort who, when seated in the back of my parents' car, stretched and twisted serpent-like to observe children sitting in other cars and agonized over the unknowability of the lives flashing by.

I have felt that Ron and I might have passed each other a handful of times over the years. On a Midtown Manhattan street in the long, cool, shadow of the green-glassed walls of Lever House; as teenagers in Jerusalem making our way through dry wadis to the old city for breakfast cooked by the Arab baker in his massive stone oven redolent of the eggplant baked that morning for the village women who had no ovens of their own; in Maine as adults bound by our parents' splintered Holocaust psyches until our own longings were dwarfed and subdued. And finally, tethered to our children in the village-greened towns of Connecticut, where the sweetness of air in spring and the sharp cut of winter's breath on ice promised perfect lives for our families.

With each almost-encounter, our paths seemed to follow an arc of intentionality through time and space until the last of these quasi meetings when, like a slowly retracting yo-yo, we moved to a gravitational field of our own.

CHAPTER 17

THE COUNTRY LIFE
(MID-1990s)

Brian and I could afford the rent on a 200-year-old house with a half-finished renovation a town away from the one he had grown up in. The white clapboard was bordered by flowering bushes and creatures with many legs, and Noah was delighted by what he found there in the dirt. "Look, Mama, Mr. Paterkillar."

The house was elegant in parts but off in others, like a painting abandoned midway. It sat close to a road that cut through town and continued north to Massachusetts. Owned last by an enterprising real estate investor who'd had bad timing, the house was repossessed by the bank when the real estate market collapsed in the late 1980s. It was next bought at auction at a steep discount by yet another investor who divided the house into two apartments.

A young couple with an air of entitled satisfaction occupied the other half. One day I brought the wife a package the mail carrier had given me, and the young woman, looking someplace to the left of my cheek, said, "We won't be here long. We need to own."

I was alarmed. Do we need to own too?

The kitchen had been worked on but not completed when the owner's money troubles began. Fleur-de-lis tiles for the backsplash, and a center island where I'd prop up Cal to give him antibiotic drops for his ear infections. My regret began then in earnest—if I had nursed him longer, he would have been healthier.

The stairway leading to the second floor was narrow, tucked in between the walls, with steep risers that scared me when I came down the steps carrying the boys. I walked uncharacteristically carefully then. The peeling paint inside the house also frightened me. Cal was crawling, and I thought there might be lead in the paint chips that fell to the floor.

After I gave birth, my fears revolved around safety. I had dreams that I left infant Noah on a bus or on a counter in a department store. Terrified that someone would take my children, I taught them to be wary of strangers. When we shopped, they squirmed, trying to ease from the iron grasp of my hand. At home, I barricaded the stairs lest they fall. Ipecac syrup for accidental poisoning was tucked away, and the telephone numbers of pediatricians were on the refrigerator.

As soon as the boys began to crawl, I insisted that my parents install safety bars on their apartment windows in Brooklyn. A blemish or bump on Noah or Cal would warrant an immediate trip to the doctor. I exhausted myself emotionally, but the constant flow of adrenaline made me think that I was fine.

Within a few months, Brian had become comfortable in his new job, and we bought a house a short walk from the one he had been raised in. I had just received a massive hat order from a new hotel casino gift shop, which provided the down payment. There was enough left over to pay off credit card debts so we could qualify for a mortgage.

Brian wanted the boys to experience his own childhood with woods and soccer fields and working farms. Close to the house was the country club where Brian had learned who the alpha males were while playing golf and caddying for pocket money. The house with its four bedrooms seemed huge to me but was a modest version of my mother-in-law's home. I was proud, a homeowner who belonged in this town, the sort of place I had longed for, that had called to me since childhood.

Stout forsythia and bougainvillea bushes in pinks and purples edged the front of the house like lace, and the driveway was a long curve of silver-gray gravel that led to the garage and backyard. I first saw the house from the road and thought it beautiful. It was a center-hall colonial, painted barn-red, and spoke of the picture-book family life that could be found inside.

The house had been built in the mid-1960s when the town was transforming itself and its acres of farmland into an affluent bedroom community for the executives who kept Hartford's burgeoning insurance industry aloft. Set about a hundred feet from a quiet, circular road on an asymmetrical mossy acre, the house was shielded from the sun by the swell of birch and oak trees. We never could keep a lawn alive because the sun could not find the grass through the trees, but I longed for one because it would have completed the picture.

On the worst days when the beauty of the landscape clashed with the ugliness inside the red house, I called upon the encounter at the hotel in Maine. Like a stubborn scent, the memory drifted in and out of the battleground of my marriage. The memory of the silent exchange with Ron became a totem with the power to resuscitate and propel me to another universe.

Inevitably when my impressions from that afternoon in Kennebunkport faded, the lines and bones of Ron's face blurring, I could still see the depth in his eyes, and I could feel what had happened between us in the air that surrounded me. Thoughts of him, and who I might have been with him, were like a vapor seeping into my atmosphere. Sometimes he was deep in my dreams, inaccessible, a possibility that had come too soon. It could have become impoverished, this memory, but the part of it that held the promise of such unimagined joy became intensely colored, and it was my secret.

Once settled in Bethel, Brian wanted to buy things—membership to the country club that had recently declined to admit Jews, a pool table, a gazebo for the front of our house. We struggled for money; we struggled with each other; there was no peace.

And Samcaps was no longer a joy. My beloved company had become a merry-go-round dependent on cash flow and the loyalty of manufacturers who always seemed to be on the verge of bumping me for an order from a mega retailer. There had also been a change in operations at the hat factory, my bedrock. Dennis developed a problem with his heart and moved with his family to a more peaceful existence in the Midwest. Uncle Seymour, whose gruffly laminated heart had brought such comfort to me, had already retired. The day-to-day management was now steered by Seymour's son. A humorless man, he hoped to increase profits by instituting new payment terms for customers who, unlike me, had been with Seymour for decades. He had no interest in preserving my extremely favorable terms—I paid Dennis when I was paid by my customers—and demanded that I pay after fourteen days. Cash flow had been something I had learned to balance surgically, and since I had no cash in reserve, this effectively put an end to Samcaps. But I was proud of my work, and one of my hats had even been photographed for a *Vogue* magazine cover.

I was ready to move on from my company, and this time the children were the force behind the choice of my next career. I became a real estate agent so my time would be my own. I could see clients and still be available to attend to the needs of Noah and Cal. I could attend school plays and classroom events. I could take the children to soccer and baseball practice and doctors' appointments.

And we also had our au pairs, Claudia first and then Heike, to help. They were from Germany—strong, delightful girls who gave their hearts to Noah and Cal. I could spend time forging relationships with clients in peace. My business and social work skills were important in this new work. It all came together and met my needs for action, human engagement, and negotiation.

But things could go bad quickly at home. If I made an offhand remark with an edge of frustration, it could cause Brian to erupt. Sometimes at night, I would leave the house and drive to Brian's mother's new apartment in Farmington, where we would talk and drink tea. I never told Sally that Brian had hurt me, but she always managed to comfort me as if she knew. Once, she hinted that Brian's father's temper had been a problem when they were married. Hesitantly she asked if Brian had ever hit me. I told her he had not. I could not allow anyone to know—I was far too ashamed. Yet I thought that she could advise me without a confession, that she would know what he had done because he was her son.

Brian's parents had met in 1954 on a train traveling east from St. Paul. It was early spring, and Sally was moving to New York to begin working as a wedding contributor for a national women's magazine. Brian's father, Don, armed with a new MBA from the University of Wisconsin, was headed to the executive training program of Sunbeam appliances. The three brothers he left behind in Madison were rarely thought or spoken about, and Brian and his sisters joked that they did not know the names of their cousins. They knew that their father's relationship with his brothers had been unpleasantly competitive.

But Brian's mother spoke openly about her youth, her voice taking us both back there. Sally's descriptions were so rich that scenes played in my head, conjuring stories I had read of bucolic Midwestern farms in the first decades of the twentieth century. She spoke with respect of her protected girlhood, the word itself so old-fashioned it evoked a vague collage of silken curls, beautifully sashed pastel dresses, and wide front porches.

I would sit on the peach swirl carpeted floor of her living room, which was furnished with early American reproductions. Sally sat on the sofa, also peach, and talked about the mother she had not known. She had been raised in St. Paul, loved and spoiled, in the sweetest ways possible by her aunt Julia and maternal grandparents. These three raised Sally with love—and I think some guilt—after her mother died days after giving birth. The death was followed by the heartbreak of all and then the flight of Sally's father, a firefighter. He had become unhinged by grief at the loss of his wife and could not accept fatherhood.

Sally's manner and expressions belied her true character; she was brighter and more resourceful than her scattered appearance suggested. She was a loving and affectionate mother, yet I often felt that she was not completely connected to anything, not even her children, as if with her mother's death Sally's ability for attachment and the desire to utterly surrender to devotion had been drained from her.

The wedding was hastened and Sally gave birth to Brian less than a year later. Two daughters followed. There were no wedding photos at their home, and I think that the children understood the absence of markers of the ceremony to be a natural result of elopement. Brian's sisters knew that their weddings would be different because their mother told them so. Their father loved the girls deeply; the youngest, Christine, was his favorite. Brian, the firstborn and perhaps the reason for the marriage, was usually an afterthought. I wonder what sort of man he would have been had he felt his father's love. I often thought that the violence was, in part, a consequence of a kind of neglect. Don traveled a good deal for work and I was told he had not attended his son's Little League baseball games. When I came to know Don, I saw few instances of genuine respect, or acknowledgement of Brian's accomplishments.

Brian seemed less aware than I was of his position in the family, reflected in the annual Christmas gathering. One after the other, his sisters would pluck their gifts from the pile under the tree. Despite his parents' divorce and its unpleasantness, Brian's parents were usually both in attendance—at least during my tenure. The girls' gifts from their father were beautifully wrapped large white boxes from old Fifth Avenue department stores. The boxes usually contained a dress made of silk or a pastel cashmere sweater, and in the case of Christine, perhaps a business suit. The size was always right.

When it was Brian's turn, I detested them all. Invariably he was given an item of clothing bought at an obscure New England outlet store of a well-known brand. A shirt or a sweater— Brian might try to return it, only to be told that the item either had not been purchased at the shop or was years old and now a drastic markdown. I felt the humiliation that Brian was supposed to feel but never seemed to, as an assault. Why couldn't Don understand how much his son had needed to be acknowledged as important by his father?

Yet in the beginning, Christmas had been a seduction. Before we married, the celebrations were small, just Brian, his mother and me, and the atmosphere in the house felt warm and loving. Brian's mother and I had taken to each other quickly and she was delighted to have someone listen so avidly to the stories of her Midwest youth, her career as a wedding consultant, and the goings-on in the lives of her friends.

Sally's Christmas tree had camouflaged boxes with my name written on the festive wrapping paper. This felt strange because as a child I had coveted Christmas, and suddenly it was mine to share in. When I was growing up, the season made everything come alive, and the streets and dressed-up store windows and even the people all seemed to shine. Our neighbors had decorated their houses competitively with glorious lights strung along every exterior plane, and Santa Claus and his reindeer resting on the front lawn were draped in strands of flashing light bulbs. I would watch from our living room window for the moment someone would flick a switch and a house would explode into a stratospheric light show. The season was, for me, light and joy rather than an expression of religious faith, and I was ravenous for it. But there was no closure—no gifts, no eggnog, no tree trimming, and the end of the season would leave me feeling empty and wanting.

At my first Christmas celebration with Brian's family, he gave me presents that spoke of a future together. There was a red ski suit, leather gloves, a scarf, ski goggles, a wallet. Brian loved Christmas and let me know that I would also love it. I began to see how easily I could slip into this non-Jewish universe. But as I tore off the wrapping paper, I was needled briefly by the absence of any effort to connect to the spiritual significance of the day. I was curious about midnight mass; I had heard of its beauty. The possibility of attending church was mentioned, but nothing came of the suggestion and it was forgotten.

The tree that Brian had chosen at a nearby farm was decorated with Sally's precious collection of ornaments which were retrieved from the attic amid her calls to be careful as we handled the delicate pieces of glass and metal. And finally, there was creamy eggnog to drink! It was delicious but heavy, and two sips were enough.

With no visits to church or allusions to whose birthday it was, and only knowing Christmas from a place of childish desire, I was not sure exactly how to integrate the experience now that it was happening. Christmas was one of the few times I felt spoiled by Brian and his mother, and that was wonderful. His world had so much glitter and light! Neither guilt nor grief seemed to be hidden in the recesses of their minds. Later, after we began to share our finances, I found out that Brian, like many, had paid for most of his purchases with his credit card, but each month he paid only the minimum and the balance and interest grew steadily.

After a few years in Bethel, we expanded our house by adding a family room in the shape of a hexagon. The addition could be seen from the street, and that was important to Brian. We paid for the renovation by refinancing our mortgage. I was anxious about the higher monthly payments, but I was having success as a real estate agent, and I knew the house would be more valuable when it was time to sell. But Brian always wanted more, and I felt like I was running on a hamster wheel.

We bought furniture from trendy shops at the mall, including a pool table, which we fought over because it was expensive and swallowed up the living room. I gave in, thinking that the pool table would bring Brian's friends to the house and he and the children would have an experience beyond what could be measured in credit card debt.

At the prospect of a new acquisition or even while simply researching one, Brian's mood elevated, and he became cheerful and upbeat. He laughed, he looked into my eyes when we spoke, and of this Brian I always wanted more. So, weekends might be spent looking at vacation houses with realtors or visiting Mercedes car showrooms. Or sometimes a trip to the mall and a small purchase at Pottery Barn sufficed. I too wanted things, but they were more along the lines of a kitchen remodel or violin and swimming lessons for the boys. Money never flowed the way we needed it to, always leaking out faster than it came in. By our second year in Connecticut, I had been earning more than Brian and he joined the country club. I was distrustful of the place because of the aura of anti-Semitism which still hung over it. The cost of initiation and monthly membership fees was high, but the club held great meaning for Brian. I thought that if he could play as much golf as he wanted, in this place of innocent boyhood where he had been most at peace, then maybe the wounds and insults of his childhood would mend.

Brian had projected that the monthly cost for the club, or "green" fees, would be a few hundred dollars. The actual number was usually more than three times that. The invoice, mailed at the end of each month, was printed on heavy cream-colored paper, the kind used for wedding invitations, with lettering that bordered on calligraphy. Maybe the bookkeeping department thought that the elegance would soften the blow and perhaps evoke an aristocratic lifestyle that was more than worth the bloated sum at the bottom of the page. That total would cause me to wake before five o'clock in the morning when sleep was banished by the anxiety of calculating from which Peter or Paul I would snatch the money to pay the bill. If I was unlucky that month, the envelope would be heavier than usual and there would be more than one page of charges. The amount, sometimes in the four figures, was printed at the bottom of a long list: golf shirts from the pro shop, beers for the guys at the bar, my own occasional client lunch in the darkly wallpapered, mostly deserted dining room.

But I put my foot down when Brian wanted to have a gazebo built in the front yard. From a financial perspective, it would not raise the value of the property, and I could not for the life of me figure out what we would do in a gazebo. Would we stand in it? Walk through it while wearing white linen outfits? I stood firm, which was always tough because Brian would scream and hurl obscenities when his plans were thwarted. Still, I said that we had more pressing things to spend money on. Money that we did not have and which would be added to the mounting credit card debt.

"The boys should have music lessons, Brian. I can't keep asking my parents to pay for these things." My father's greatest pleasure, after my mother, was classical music. He would be in heaven if the boys studied the violin, and I wanted to give that to him.

"They have plenty of money and that's what they like to do with it," Brian said. He was interested in my parents' financial situation and knew that they would not hold anything back that could enrich the lives of their grandchildren.

My parents' situation had changed in the early 1980s after my father quit his job as an elevator designer. He had been working during the day and studying for a master's degree in business at night until one day he walked out of his office and called my mother from a pay phone on the street. She was concerned when she heard his voice; it was unlike him to call during the day unless there was a problem.

"What is it, Eddie?" she asked.

"I can't take it anymore," he said sorrowfully.

My mother, knowing his frustrations at this place, the nasty behavior of the bosses who had heaped dozens of small acts of indignity on my father, did not skip a beat. "Leave," she said.

"Leave now. It's enough. They don't deserve you. You'll find something else where they will treat you like a human being."

"But the money! You're not working now—what will we do?"

"I can go back to substitute teaching, and you can, too, until you finish your MBA. Then you'll find a real job. You can't stay there anymore, Eddie. It's eating you up alive. Tell them you're leaving, or don't. Just come home."

It was 1980, and my father never went back to his job. Instead, he pulled together whatever money he could find, borrowed some more from Aunt Frieda—who was looking for a solid investment after she received her long-anticipated divorce settlement—and bought a hundred-year-old lime-stone building with ten studio apartments on the western edge of Central Park in Manhattan. The building was a beauty from old New York's Beaux Arts period, but my father, now unemployed, did not qualify for a conventional mortgage. Instead, he took a loan at a double-digit interest rate from the seller of the property, who, as a convicted felon recently released from prison, had managed to hold onto his only asset.

My mother was more conservative than my father and would have had a problem with this purchase had she not been recuperating in the hospital following a foot operation. To ease her pain, she had been given generous amounts of morphine, so she did not think anything of it when my dad pushed some papers at her to sign.

The seller, a burly, fast-talking guy, insisted we call him "Uncle Louie," his prison moniker. He wore a large cowboy hat and hung around the street, usually in the company of a sweet-looking young man we assumed was his boyfriend. In addition to the usurious interest rate, another problem was that Uncle Louie continued to try to collect rent from the tenants after he sold the building to my parents.

I had been living in the cheapest apartment in the building (until the day I was robbed and returned home to Brooklyn), and I called my father one afternoon. "Dad, you own the building, right?"

"Of course, what's wrong with you? What kind of a question is that!"

"Well, Uncle Louie is here, knocking on doors and asking for rent money."

To address this sort of sketchy behavior and any other problem that came up suddenly, such as an electrical outage, basement flood, or strange animal making an appearance, my dad would jump on the subway and with a restraint that I had never seen in him before, resolve most any disaster. We could not afford to hire a handyman to watch over and care for the building, so my father took on that job and became intimate with the goings-on in the basement and the animals, birds, and bugs who nested there. He enjoyed watching me and my mother scream and shudder as he described the lives of these creatures.

A few years later, my dad negotiated the sale of the building and two more adjacent to it. The package was sold to a group of Turkish developers. He sold the building for nearly ten times the price he had paid. After that, my parents invested in lower-maintenance real estate. Despite the fact that they still lived in their one-bedroom Brooklyn apartment for another decade until moving to a Manhattan apartment with Central Park views, we all knew that everything had changed and the days of worrying about money were over.

Back in the red house, I said, "Brian, we can't take money that we need for the boys and build a gazebo that has no possible use!"

"Who the hell do you think you are, talking to me like that? You think I'm going to live like a loser? Like that guy

Alex I went to high school with over on Country Club Road? His house looks like a shithole, and everyone knows it!"

Brian was referring to a man who worked as a police officer in town. Alex and his wife had several children, and I'd heard he took every minute of overtime he could get. Sometimes I saw him at the supermarket or bagel shop, always with a couple of kids, and I yearned for what I saw in this stranger; he seemed to glow with devotion to his family.

But Brian was free with my parents' money; he knew that they would deny Cal and Noah nothing. They paid for nursery school, swimming lessons, clothes, a trip to Disney World. One winter, my parents asked me to order jackets from a clothing catalog for the boys. Brian was a fan of its preppy style and wanted to order something for himself.

"Just give them the total amount. They'll think it was for the kids."

Such a small thing, a comment only, but it was as if an explosive device had flown from his mouth. I can still see Brian standing casually, comfortably next to the black wood-burning stove, the exposed brick wall behind him as he spoke. The boys played on the sofa in front of the large window with its view of the backyard and swing set. It was night and the back light cast a yellow glow over the deck with its mahogany boards. It was all so lovely to see, yet I wanted only to melt into the ground because I knew then that the marriage was over.

Brian's casual suggestion that I deceive my parents, just as they were expressing their love, had exposed his utter disregard for my core values—trust, loyalty, and honesty—and left me knowing that I could no longer be with him. I knew separation would devastate the children; it was the one fact of divorce that had kept me from considering it previously. The sense of being split apart by my desperately warring emotions dissipated as my resolve grew stronger.

For all the outward loveliness of Brian's world, I learned finally that although I could be immersed in its beauty, I had never had access to anyone's heart. And in time, the beauty became oppressive and the falseness louder and more overwhelming than the clamor of any city, and I longed for human noise and grit.

CHAPTER 18

LEAVING

Five years after leaving New York, I suddenly felt, with a great sense of urgency, that time was passing quickly. I was forty-three years old and the measure of years I had lived began to have increasing meaning, as if it marked the halfway point of my life. And so I made an agreement with myself: I would not walk the second half of my life with Brian. The ten-day road trip we had just taken halfway across the country had failed to achieve its purpose of fixing the ruin of our marriage. The boys had been happily ensconced with my parents in Brooklyn as Brian and I drove west to visit St. Paul, the city his mother had grown up in. I was excited to see the places where Sally's stories had played out, thinking that this foray into Brian's roots could bring us closer and give us something meaningful to share.

Our conversation during the days on the road was stilted. Alone now without the buffer provided by our children, we had little to say to each other. I felt encapsulated in the car, and it seemed like a microcosm of my marriage. To stay with Brian would mean I would be trapped for the rest of my days, forever breathing in the recirculated air of a false life. Brian had not seemed very interested in the early years of his mother, nor was he curious about the lives of his great grandparents who had raised Sally. I could not wait to get back to my children.

When we returned home, there was still much mental work to be done in reaching the next step in my *mind*. I did not tell my parents what I now knew would be happening because I could not predict when the conclusions in my head would be translated into actions. Yet there was no questioning, no more prevarication, just the settled knowledge that this part of my life was over and that careful logistics would be necessary to shield the children as best I could. I set about trying to advance my thinking and to plan for the rupture. I was certain that the impact on the boys' lives would be brutal, but I pushed myself to pack those thoughts away so that I could proceed. My children would be children of divorce, and there was not a thing I could do to prevent it. The old cliché was correct: If I stayed, it would be worse for my boys.

I became primed to leave, and the emotional act of giving up my marriage and calling it out as failed snapped the bonds that had held my denial in place. Suddenly I had the freedom to see things as they were. With this realization, the impact of the hand I had been dealt as a child of Holocaust survivors also weakened; I was not a prisoner.

This understanding became the layer of insulation that protected me from the marriage's ongoing insults, leaving me less vulnerable to Brian. It also made the debris around me more obvious. I was no longer a reactive participant—I could observe. As I started to visualize leaving, I was euphoric. But reality insinuated its way in—where would we live, how would Brian react, how would we manage financially, what would my parents say? By elucidating to myself the likely sequence of events involved in ending our marriage I could prepare myself, at least intellectually, for the upheavals that would follow.

What remained was to shore up my strength for the coming onslaught; the rest I could not anticipate.

I did not end my marriage because Brian had hurt me. In the year before my unhappiness had coalesced into a resolve to leave, I had begun to awaken in the middle of the night. Like a desert nomad, I wandered around our bedroom, still as much asleep as awake, while Brian slept. I should have felt tenderness for his vulnerability, but I was filled instead with the fear that a malignancy had infiltrated my being. It was on one of these nights that I realized I could not spend the rest of my life with Brian. I felt it then as a matter of character, of dissonant values, yet hadn't I seen more than enough glimpses into his character before we were married? At that time, I had seen failure ahead yet pressed on, and nine years later failure had arrived. Looking back, I don't like what my actions say about *my* character. Brian had deserved honesty, but when I married him I had such a meager understanding of my own motivations that honesty was impossible.

The beatings did not figure in a significant way in my decision to leave, the last one having taken place three years before. That time, it was late at night, and I believed that the children, asleep, had heard nothing. I had provoked Brian by commenting that one of his friends-who had mocked Jewish customs- was anti-Semitic.

Too late, I saw the tensing and drawing in of his face and knew it was going to happen again. In utter despair, enraged at myself, I twisted my glasses. They broke easily, and as I held the now useless glasses in my hands, I felt great relief, as if my bad behavior proved my complicity and could make me believe I was as responsible as Brian. I had to see this horror as a mutuality, a symbiosis, that we were two crazy people who needed chaos to function. The realization that I was victimized by Brian was unbearable, and it would have required me to leave him earlier, before I was ready.

As Brian banged the back of my head into the closet doors, I was grateful that it was not the more solid wall that he had pushed me up against. I became pliant and made my body rag-like as he pushed and pulled me by the shoulders. I never fought back, and I have never been certain why. I think that I knew it would end sooner if I allowed it to run its course, as if Brian needed to do this for some physiological reason. I also knew that he never seemed to use all his strength, and I feared that fighting back would fuel his rage. And there was still my feeling that this was what I deserved.

After it was over, I went downstairs to the family room to sleep, frightened that the children had heard us—that they would now learn the true relationship between their parents and the knowledge would break them. In the morning before seven o'clock, Brian came to me. I was pretending to be asleep, which he might have sensed. He was hesitant as he slipped into the room; he seemed scared and on edge, as if this time he knew he had gone too far. As I opened my eyes just enough to see, he came close and checked my face and jaw for bruises. Satisfied that they were minor, he left to keep his golf game tee-time at the country club.

I knew that I had to stop Brian from attacking me again because the children were getting older and it was just a matter of time until they would wake and see us. When Brian came home that afternoon, I kept a distance from him. I did not flinch as I told him that if he ever touched me again, I would go to the school where he worked, and to the police, and I would take the children back to New York. He believed me, and from then on everything vile between us was verbal rather than physical.

With the waning of my emotional connection to Brian, my awareness of the true nature of our marriage became sharper and I watched the moments of our life attentively. A few incidents stood out.

One afternoon in the early spring, Brian came home with Noah after playing tennis. Noah was quiet and more reserved than usual. He arranged his small body in the deep armchair next to the sofa where his father sat. Brian, in language that seemed too mature for a child of six, began to explain that he had slapped Noah on the tennis court. He said he had done this because he became frustrated when Noah, who was six, hadn't seemed fully engaged in Brian's tutorial.

I remember Noah's legs sticking out from the cushion of the deep chair and his eyes looking straight ahead toward the wood-burning stove. Brian said he should not have gotten so angry, but he was stressed by Noah's not taking the game seriously enough. I saw then how I had deluded myself by wanting to believe the boys could grow up free of Brian's violence.

Another incident took place shortly afterward. On a bright Saturday morning, parents stood on the perimeter of a soccer field cheering their children, still so small, huddling in their soccer gear. The game started, and an error was made. I remember Brian's balled-up fists rigid at his sides as he rushed the field, the wide-eyed players scrambling to get out of his way as he delivered a hand-waving diatribe to the referee, the players, our boys. I felt the sting of mortification, and a voice screamed in my head that since I *knew* what Brian was capable of, being married to him made me his enabler. But if Brian could not control this part of himself, this place of hurt formed so long ago, what was my responsibility as his wife?

When his outburst subsided, it was silent on the field, and Brian stood with his feet planted in the grass, still vibrating with anger. Confusion came to his face as the crowd stared. He was alone and I did not go to him.

The coach ordered Brian off the soccer field and told him not to come back, that he was scaring the children. In the backseat of the car, the boys were silent as Brian ranted about the coach's bias, his untoward reaction, the fact that children needed to learn! He had no idea how he was perceived. I looked straight ahead so I would not have to meet the eyes of other parents, and I spoke meaningless words of understanding. I hated myself then.

A third incident further intensified my resolve to end the marriage. It occurred during a visit to pay our respects at the home of the newly widowed father of Brian's brother-in-law. Exploring, I marveled at the ragtag luxury of the house, which sprawled elegantly and was set on several acres in a part of Long Island that had no need for a kosher butcher. The boys were with my parents, and I wandered alone through the house feeling strangely unencumbered and light, a sweet sensation.

Walking outside, I came upon Brian in the shaded stone garden as he held court with several of his brother-in-law's friends. He was discussing a book he was reading about New Age spirituality. As I listened to him speak, something caustic moved into my throat. In my mind's eye, the beatings formed a backdrop to Brian's earnest descriptions of the book's life-changing principles. As I stood at the edge of the group, I was sharply aware of the poverty of Brian's being.

The last incident was the one that I have never recovered from. We were driving to Cape Cod to spend a week with Brian's sisters and their families during the summer of 1997, before we separated. The boys' beloved au pair Claudia was visiting from Germany and was in the car with us. Noah and Cal were thrilled to be with her again, happily sitting in the backseat with her.

We stopped for a bathroom break at a rest stop on the Massachusetts Turnpike. It was a massive place with a gas station, several fast-food chains, and souvenir shops. Hundreds of people milled about. Brian took the boys into the huge men's restroom, and I luxuriated for a few minutes alone in the women's restroom, dawdling in front of the mirror. When I came out to face what I was certain would be Brian's annoyed expression, he and the boys were not there.

When Brian finally emerged from the men's restroom alone, his face was contorted with fear and he was wringing his hands oddly as if rinsing them over and over. In his eyes were the words that hadn't yet formed on his lips. I ran past him and dropped to my knees, crawling the length of the restroom floor while calling out for the boys.

Brian followed me. "They were in the next stall," he said. "I had to pee so bad, I don't know what happened!"

Moving on my hands and knees from stall to stall, I felt sick from terror and the foul dankness of the floor. I had, in seconds, fallen from this world to another where any physical or other awareness of my corporeal being vanished along with the children. I become a thing of pure energy, of non-matter. Until I saw my boys, saw the volumes of their flesh fill up space, their bodies pushing the air aside, I was no longer part of the physical world.

I watched myself running, shouting to anyone I saw, "Have you seen two little boys?"

I turned away from these strangers as soon as their faces registered perplexity, sympathy, or the worst, a wince of relief that they were not in my shoes. I looked for other faces whose mouths would smile and say, "Yes, they just walked by! There they are!" They would point to Noah and Cal, and I would deflate and fall to the ground. Pressing myself into the earth, I would become a person again.

But no one had seen them. I approached our car from the rear and as I moved closer, I thought that I was seeing an apparition. Through the dust of the back window, I made out something sticking up from one of the car seats. It was a head! I rushed to the rear door and saw both boys sitting calmly next to Claudia.

Noah, at five, had taken his four-year-old brother's hand and together they crossed the lanes packed with eighteen-wheel trucks waiting to fill up their gas tanks. Noah said they had called to their father when they were finished in the restroom, but he had not answered, so they decided to leave. I stopped shaking around the time we arrived at the vacation house we had rented, but the horror of that day still lives inside me.

The next morning, I was walking across the beach with Cal in my arms to retrieve toys that had been left behind, while Brian was supposed to watch Noah playing at the water's edge. Chatting with his sister, Brian apparently became distracted. Noah, not trusting that I would bring back all the toys, left the family group and followed me in silence for half a mile before reaching out his hand to touch my back.

Shocked, I whirled around to see my son standing there. As Noah sheepishly admitted his concerns for the safety of the toys, Brian appeared, panting from running on the sand, shaken and visibly relieved to see Noah. While I had been peacefully oblivious, he had been petrified that Noah had disappeared into the water.

Having made the decision to leave him, I was not exactly sure how to do it. One morning Brian called me from work, angry because I had not done something he had asked me to take care of. He spoke quietly—there were people around him—but his voice was tight and laced with frustration. "I've had enough of this, Rena. You're not giving me what I need in this marriage... what I deserve! Do you even think about what I do for our family? I am not getting what I need to feel valued!"

In that moment, I could feel a part of our dynamic shift. Brian's rage was uncharacteristically muted, and the boys were at school, so I was not flooded by terror that they might hear us. As I raised my voice, with a great *whoosh* my lungs emptied and I felt an enormous rush of relief. I replied, "Brian, there is no more. I have no more. You've taken everything, more than everything. I will not give you more because then I'll have to start taking from the boys and I won't do that."

He was silent for a few seconds and then, almost in a tone of indifference, he said, "Well, it's pointless for us to continue like this if you aren't going to change."

My chest—I always felt freedom in the expansiveness of my breath—opened wide. I told him he was right, said good-bye, and hung up. A few days passed, a sort of purgatory in that Brian did not speak to me unless it was absolutely necessary. We had planned to be in New York that weekend and we kept to the schedule.

By then we agreed to continue to talk, and with my parents babysitting, Brian and I ate dinner that night at Monte's, a storied old Italian restaurant in Greenwich Village. The waiters were all men, professionals, and the tables were covered with white cloths laid down twice. It was a restaurant I loved, a place where history spoke from all corners of the mahogany-lined dining room. We sat at a table for two facing each other, and I felt laid bare, suddenly struck by a flash of hope. I wanted so much to bring Brian into the hopeful space that had just opened, and I told him what I saw of us and the leaps that we would need to take to stay together.

Brian was calm, wearing his public persona, and he gave an analysis of our marital situation, which was a continuation of the telephone conversation minus the rage. He spoke clinically: "Look, we're just not suited for each other anymore. I need more from a relationship than you're capable of giving."

"What exactly do you need, Brian?"

"I need your attention. You're always preoccupied with the boys, school, and your work. I need you to be focused on me too!"

What Brian asked for should have been natural for me to give. But the years of struggle had turned my love—my ability to care for him—into something with limits, and whatever I had of this intangible stuff would go to my children. After ten years, I felt very little empathy for this man. It was a tragedy for both of us. Yet, despite what he was saying, I felt such an openness that if Brian had done *anything* to show that he wanted to keep our family whole, I would have stayed.

I think that my sudden change of heart was due to a mounting visceral fear of the inevitable—the fracture of our family. And because our boys would be left helpless in its wake, I was desperate for a last Hail Mary to sidestep that grief.

A heaviness swept through me, bolting me to the chair as my body gave over to gravity; my arms were weighted down by the hands in my lap. Cal and Noah were losing something elemental and completely taken for granted, like an arm or leg. An anchor of childhood would soon shatter, one they would forever notice intact in others. I began to cry, embarrassing myself. Brian did not comment or attempt to touch me.

The waiter brought our meals. He was flushed and lumbering, a worn-out man. I wondered how he could see, so hidden were his eyes by his drooping lids, the lower half of his face fading into his neck. I thought he would understand what I was feeling. The eggplant I ordered was served in the pan in which it had been baked. The cheese bubbled brown and gold at the edges.

I was hungry, but the knowledge of how to eat was lost to me. It was not possible to lift the fork to my mouth. I wept for the sorrow of having to dismember a family. I wept for my boys who were going to be children with parents who lived apart. I wept because now there was no going back, no impetus to stay. My tears fell and slid off the now-hardened cheese. I stared down the pain; I knew what I had to do.

We returned to Connecticut the next day. We said little to each other in the car. I slept downstairs that night and the next. The second morning, waking before dawn, I left the house and drove to my office in Simsbury, stopping first to buy cigarettes. When I was younger, I had smoked for a few years, mostly when I drank wine. I pulled the car into the empty office parking lot and called my parents. We spoke for about an hour.

Smoking one cigarette after another, I emptied half of the pack during the conversation. I told my mother and father, each one on a phone extension, that I had decided to leave Brian. I also told them about the beatings. They had not known; no one did. In the sounds that came through the phone, I heard my father's shock and my mother's anguish.

The trip from my parents' Brooklyn apartment to the house in Connecticut normally took more than two hours without traffic, but ninety minutes later they arrived with packed suitcases. They knew this would not be a short visit. For my parents, this moment had been longed for, albeit ambivalently, since they had first met Brian ten years earlier.

PART II

CHAPTER 19

A RESPITE AND RENEWAL

The boys were overjoyed at the sudden early-morning appearance of their grandparents and jumped up and down, yelling wildly. Brian was taken aback. My parents dressed the boys and took them out for breakfast.

I had an hour to talk with Brian. I told him I was leaving with Noah and Cal for a short trip. "We need to think, both of us. We need to make some plans," I said.

He stared at my face. He hadn't taken me seriously, I realized.

"No, Rena, no," he said, taking my arm. "You don't have to go. You *shouldn't* go! Everything is okay. I realized it all this morning—how much I love you. We are a family. We need to stay together and work through this. We have to—for the boys!"

But I was no longer open to the possibility of staying, and in the manner of someone who by departing is pulverizing the life of another, I tried to limit the wounds I caused. I spoke to him kindly, feeling the lure of the escape that was finally certain and at hand. His rising panic was an impediment to get past so I could leave with my children. To my mind, we had severed our marriage officially at the dinner in New York. Now I focused only on extricating myself.

Brian spoke with reverence and passion about family, the boys, and our history. He began to perspire and his face reddened. I did not argue, I listened, my eyes trained on his face as I calculated when his face would contort with rage. He was not used to the calm I was projecting and began to smell danger, exposing his fear.

"I was upset last night," he said. "I... I just wasn't thinking straight." He was waving his hands. "Okay, I'm going to be very honest. I'm sorry I did this—it was wrong. I made a mistake. I felt that if you thought I was unhappy enough to end things—us—that you would give me more. But I see now that you give so much. You're such a good mother, Rena. Please forgive me for doing this. Please, let's—"

I interrupted, "Brian, I understand what you're saying, but still—even if that's why you said those things—there is unhappiness here, for both of us. This is right; I think you know it is."

"No!" he shot back. "Let's just forget this. Please. Let's not be insane. This is our home, our marriage, our family."

I was not surprised by his confession. I was thankful and relieved for Brian's duplicity. I needed to get out of the house with the boys, and I would have said anything then to do it.

"Look, Brian, this is so hard. I'll take the boys for a short trip, a little vacation for the boys with my parents. We can talk every day. And we will figure out what to do."

"But why do you need to go away to think? We can talk together. Here. We can process this together. You don't need to go!"

"I do need to. But I'll be back in a week and you'll speak to the boys on the phone every day."

Brian sank into a chair and cried.

Still standing, I put my arms around him and felt the grief move through the cool cotton of his shirt. He clutched at my waist the way a child would.

In the car, the boys shook with excitement. My mother settled herself between them in the backseat and began to admonish them, only half playfully, to behave before I started the engine. Brian did not step out from the house as we prepared to leave but stood looking through the window of the family room. He was still, one hand holding the curtains aside. His face was furrowed, the long parentheses-like lines around his mouth deeper than usual.

From the back of the car the boys' high voices bubbled up, "Where are we going? How long are we staying? How far is it?"

My father sat next to me, in the passenger seat, his silent presence a reassurance like no other. I turned my focus to the road in front of us. Where would we go? We needed a place by the ocean, that much I knew. The beach and sea were like manna from heaven to my dad and the children.

Martha's Vineyard came to my mind as we drove north on the flat, treeless highway, but it was too far. I marveled that I could separate Brian from the time I had spent there and recall the island and its raw beauty with fondness. Brian had believed that we ought to have certain things—that we were entitled to them—yet he was frugal when it came to family vacations, which yielded nothing more tangible than memories. He wanted things he could wear, hold, look at, walk into, drive.

The week we would vacation on Martha's Vineyard was a tradition started by Brian and his sisters when they were in their twenties. It was usually at the end of June, and the siblings would share the rent on a simple cottage furnished only with necessities: plain wooden furniture, bunk beds, and an outdoor shower that fascinated the children. The house sat on the edge of a small bay, a perfect spot for children and their parents.

The kids merely needed to wade ankle-deep to see all manner of tiny sea creatures centrifuging up through the wet sand by the constant flow of the water. There was always one child, usually Cal, who wanted to play with the creatures while others insisted that their environment not be disturbed. But Cal was in his element by the sea. He would leave his cousins to explore, and trailing his fingers as if blind, he would emerge with shells, a fish or hermit crab ("Look, Mama, a Herman crab!") resting in a tiny pool he had made in his hand.

The adults walked through the bay, waist-high at its deepest, to the sea with the children sitting on their shoulders. Once in the ocean, the parents would alternately toss the children about and raise them high above the cold June water. The kids called to each other as tall waves fell over them in gray sheets of liquid glass. The spray ricocheted all around, infusing joy into the wild yells of the children.

The nights were especially ravishing. With nothing except the occasional small plane and light years between the stars and us, we would lie on our backs in the long grass growing out from the dunes. Cal would usually be the first to become limp from his exertions of the day. His lips and cheeks glowed red in the moonlight as he drifted off. He was still small enough to curl his body tight, and I would wrap him up in my arms. In sleep, his limbs were heavy and solid, and his fingers stretched out—searching for more ocean booty, I liked to think.

Now, behind the wheel of the car, stewarding my family somewhere unknown, I understood that it was this very innocence that I was about to smash to smithereens. I wondered whether my actions of today would forever bar from their lives the possibility of a future as free and unencumbered as the boys had experienced on Martha's Vineyard. And wasn't the warmth and sense of inclusion I had felt there about to be relegated to history?

My sisters-in-law and I used to cook together in the tiny kitchen, watch over each other's children at the beach, go into town to shop for food or get an ice cream cone. But there was an edge, something that had been off throughout my tenure with Brian's family, the impression of a line that would not be crossed. I think Brian's father, with his matter-of-fact curiosity about me—a Jew who had come into the family—had been the most honest.

The beauty of the setting on the Vineyard was such that during each visit I was moved by the possibility of familial peace and thought that maybe there was still hope for me and Brian: a way to reverse everything ugly that had accompanied our union. I hoped that the way we were on the island could become our lives. But within a couple of days, reality would creep back in and break through the idyll. Often this happened when I saw Brian interact with others. He was charmingly true to himself in public, but his truth was counterfeit and I hated how, through our marriage, his duplicity had leached onto me.

Nearly every step with Brian was fraught because no matter who we were with, what we were doing, or where we were doing it, disappointment trailed. I could never shake my underlying distrust of him and his motives. We did not share a vision of the next moment, year, or lifetime.

I came out of my reverie abruptly, realizing that along with these memories, there would be many pieces of my life with my husband that I would sadly leave behind—the casualties of divorce.

I knew that I had to start thinking about where we were going to land now. I turned the car east toward Cape Cod and saw the bottleneck of traffic on the Cape route below us.

Everything had stopped. My father produced a map from the glove compartment and began to search for alternatives.

"What about Maine?" I asked, my voice sounding rushed, barreling. I needed to have a plan, quickly, and then I remembered our long-ago overnight stay on the Maine coast.

"Kennebunkport is pretty" I said. "We were there once, just for a night when we left New York. It's small and touristy, sort of kitschy, but in a nice way. I think the boys would enjoy it. It's on the ocean, and you'd like that, Dad." I looked at him quickly, anxiously.

My father, never a big talker when he had to plan, rifled again through the glove compartment and found a New England guidebook with a list of hotels. He read aloud descriptions of a few, and one, built at the turn of the century, stood out. It had rooms facing the ocean, a saltwater pool, and gardens.

I called the hotel, and the woman who answered calmed me immediately with a slow, mellow voice that sounded like a vacation. There were no more rooms in the main hotel, she said, but there was another possibility. We could stay in an adjacent house, on the top floor where there were three bedrooms and a bathroom. We would have the whole floor to ourselves. The price seemed too low, especially because all meals were included. I was elated and thanked her several times before hanging up. She must have wondered who was coming to stay.

The Colony Hotel's façade was weathered white clapboard. There was a front porch behind a drive where cars could unload. The lobby was a horizontal sprawl with sitting areas on one side and a gift shop and dining room on the other. The rear of the hotel faced the ocean, and mahogany French doors led directly out to the garden, beyond which was the gunmetal gray of the Atlantic as it rose and dipped in a lazy rhythm. It was a green place, and the boys were delighted to find a small putting golf course set up next to the pool. Startling bursts of color were all around as flowers pushed themselves through the green; the landscaping was imprecise and thus seemed perfect to my eyes. A large pool lay off a meandering stone path on the hotel's other flank. The water in it appeared to stretch, ending just where the ocean began.

I stood quietly, taking everything in. We were here, away, somewhere safe. I felt delivered, and the heavy ocean breeze marched in through the open doors like a welcoming salute. And I knew that five years earlier, I had seen him here—the man whose eyes had transported me.

An awareness of my new autonomy surged through me. The sublime feeling was the antithesis to my marriage, which, I was realizing all day in glorious increments of comprehension, was over.

We stayed for a week, and the boys were happy. Days were spent at the pool, where Cal continued his love affair with the water. His muscular little body coiling and uncoiling, Cal stayed underwater for horrifying amounts of time before coming up for air. Noah ran around the grounds and played on the putting green with the other guests, mostly sun-dried older men who wore bright plaid pants and belts with miniature whales or ducks woven into them.

Meals were huge at the hotel—buffets that made my father and the boys crazy. Instead of having breakfast, my mother and I sipped coffee from paper cups while walking up the coastal road. We talked about the things she had never known about my marriage.

"It was strange," I said to her. "You finally stopped acting as if you couldn't stand him, and that's when I started to realize it was over." I told her that when I no longer felt burdened by having to fight their judgments, my own flowed hard and fast, no longer filtered by a need to preserve the marriage. I started to see Brian as missing something essential, something that I could not keep living without. I wasn't sure she understood or even truly heard what I was saying, because she was so caught up in not having known that Brian had hit me. She kept talking about what she would have done if she had known.

Every afternoon after lunch, which was served poolside, my father would take the boys into town for ice cream. Before leaving, he would hand me the bottle of red wine we had brought with us and a glass. I would fill the glass and call Brian. There were about six or seven of these telephone calls over the course of the week. At first Brian was gentle, speaking low and carefully. As the days progressed and I stayed firm in my decision, he became agitated and then hysterical. By the following day he seemed to have collected himself until the last conversation, when Brian discarded any pretense of understanding and raged at me.

CHAPTER 20

A PROCESS OF DISMANTLING
(1999)

The boys and I returned to Connecticut because we had to, and Brian and I went to counseling together. By then I was certain that he would not change, yet I created an unspoken proviso: if Brian found that living without me was unacceptable and he changed in several fundamental ways, I would stay to keep our family together.

I asked Brian to move out to give me space to think without his influence bearing down on me. He resisted mightily but eventually agreed to live with his mother. I needed to see him spend money on things that he, himself, would not physically benefit from—to demonstrate that he could be selfless. I wanted him to prove that he could dedicate himself to the family's well-being by paying the mortgage and electric bill even though he was not living in the house with us—that he felt the need to take care of us and to ensure that we would be safe.

In my mind, this behavior would portend a profound shift in his character and show the rearrangement of his priorities. If Brian succeeded in acting counter to his strongest impulses— if he was able to renounce his tendencies to be ungenerous, to rage, to see things from a position of entitlement—it would suggest that a metamorphosis had taken place. Pivoting to a more mature perspective would require radical growth, and if such a transformation could be sustained, I would stay with him. The first month, he left a check for the mortgage payment on the kitchen counter. Would this continue?

We went to see a psychologist Brian had found, and he told the therapist about the beatings. I was moved by his honesty. The psychologist, Paul Reid, insisted that I come alone to the next meeting. The beating that had taken place after Noah's birth concerned Dr. Reid the most. He had decided to use a treatment method that was helpful for survivors of trauma. I did not think I had PTSD, my wounds from Brian having closed long ago, even before I knew that he would no longer be my life partner. I cooperated with the psychologist because I wanted to be agreeable. When I met with Dr. Reid, he instructed me to close my eyes so he could track the eye movements beneath my eyelids as I recounted the incident that had taken place in the bathroom a few days after Noah was born. I found the whole business silly.

After a few weeks, Brian's patience frayed. He would come to the house in the evenings and push to move back home, though we had been to only one therapy session together. The second month of the separation, Brian did not make the mortgage payment and stopped paying any of our expenses. To my relief, Brian's actions signaled that it was time for me to hire a lawyer and file for divorce.

I told Brian that I wanted to move back to New York with the children. He announced that he would not allow it. Brian's rage now seemed to have few limits. When he came to the house, he was calm for just a bit until I raised the subject of our move to New York. Then he would scream at me, threatening to keep us in Connecticut or to extort my parents for money if I did not agree to fulfill additional demands.

"You think I am going to let you take my kids to New York? To live in some fancy apartment that your parents buy you?"

He smirked at me as if he had a great secret. "You better watch out," he said finally.

I was scared. What could he possibly be talking about? Watch out for what?

"You better pray I won't go after your parents' money!" He said this triumphantly, as if it were proof of his brilliance.

I laughed at him then. But it revolted me that the father of my children could be so pleased with the idea of extorting money from their grandparents.

One evening, months later, Brian tried again to convince me to give up the divorce action. I was careful not to provoke him because the children were awake. Despite my efforts to forestall his anger, he amped himself into a fury and slammed out of the house, screaming at me.

"I won't let you destroy everything! The boys need grass and a house, not a concrete playground. You won't get away with it. I will never ever let you leave the state!" He gunned the car engine hard as he sped down the gravel driveway. Amid the sounds of flying stones and screeching tires, Brian's yells invaded the house through open windows.

Noah came downstairs, conflict dulling his beautiful face. In his eyes was an ache as deep as any I had ever seen. He was seven years old and tortured. How could he make sense of what he had just heard? His world was the one we had made for him, but now it had been crumpled up and thrown into his face.

"Where did Dad go? Why was he yelling?"

"He's upset, sweetheart. He doesn't think we should be separated so he gets really frustrated and yells."

Noah stared past my shoulder through the window toward the driveway Brian had just sped down. The utter blankness of his expression—the dogged refusal to condemn either of us—was unbearable. Shouldn't he be imploring me to let his father come home?

"I am going to yell like Dad does when I'm a man," he said finally.

"No, Noah," I said. "You can take whatever you want from each of us and just leave the stuff that you don't like. It's up to you. We both have ways that are not so good, because we are human beings, and you can just toss those away. But we love you and Cal so much, and that's something that you can take from us and give to your children when you are a man."

He seemed to become less rigid then; his face relaxed and I brought him upstairs to the room he shared with Cal who, thankfully, still slept. Noah climbed into bed, and I kissed him and held him, and somehow I felt lucky.

Cal's wounds were more visible. When Brian and I first separated, he had just turned five. Cal's heart lived in the overlapping spaces of the people he loved, and when his father and I came apart, something wrenched open in him. He told his preschool teacher, "Something terrible has happened. My daddy doesn't sleep at home anymore."

Cal's words had never come easily, but he saw everything. Half-articulated thoughts dissipating like the soft end of an exhale were often finished by his brother and came less frequently now. He did not so much retreat as give up.

The fall in Connecticut was magical and short. Some afternoons, when the air was so crisp that it felt like a bite, I would drive the boys to a farm near the town soccer fields. At its entrance was a truck that cooked up apple fritters on a stove in the back; sitting in the car, we devoured them and watched the cows. In previous years, these activities with their symbolism of family harmony had felt like a mockery because they were so much at odds with the truth of my life. But now, knowing I was no longer bound to Brian and this place, I enjoyed the outings fully for the first time.

The children returned to school, and I was grateful for the small measure of normalcy it brought back to their lives. Cal started kindergarten, and I waited excitedly at the bus stop for him after his first day of school. When Cal climbed down the steps of the bus, his backpack seemed larger than the back it embraced. Walking home, he informed me that although he had enjoyed school, I must call his teacher and let her know that from then on, he would be attending only half days as he had in preschool. Foreshadowed in Cal's announcement was his lifelong need to be autonomous in almost everything he would do.

In the meantime, Brian had grown thinner, and his friends told me that he suffered over our separation. I tried to share my rosy outlook for the future, that we would still be a family, differently configured, but he would have none of it. By winter, fury was his default emotion. Night after night, he would come to the house and berate me and my plans and threaten to fight me for custody and prevent our move to New York. My lawyer told me a story, possibly divorce folklore, about a Connecticut family court judge who had kept a mother and her children from moving to the next town after the father objected. I accepted that this could happen, but I refused to concede more to Brian than I already had.

After almost a year of separation, Brian and I had finally exacted an agreement from each other and, miraculously, he let us go. I was now free to leave for New York with the boys. Although Brian's earnings as a psychologist had become substantial over the years, he refused to go along with our relocation unless I accepted child support payments of one hundred fifty dollars per child, a total of three hundred dollars per month. I also gave up any claim to alimony or to Brian's school pension.

My lawyer wrote an official letter advising me that my decisions regarding the financial aspects of the separation were neither equitable nor in my best interests. I didn't care. I wanted out of the marriage so desperately that I would have agreed to receive no support at all. I knew I could earn money. I would work in a department store if I failed in what I'd heard was the carnivorous world of New York real estate. I was depleted from the new demands that Brian came up with on his nightly visits, but on the day when my lawyer informed me that an agreement had been reached, I was overjoyed. We were going home!

My relief evaporated the next morning when the lawyer called and asked whether Brian and I had borrowed money from my parents that had not been repaid. I had forgotten that years earlier they had loaned us $30,000 for which we had signed notes along with a payment schedule. I knew that my parents would forgive the loan, but Brian demanded that his release from the debt be explicitly stated in the separation agreement.

My dad was fine with this; he just wanted us to come back home. But my mother slipped into battle mode, refusing to release Brian from the debt. She simply would not appease him as I had. I had the uncomfortable impression that she wouldn't agree to this new demand even if it meant I could not leave Connecticut. Brian was not motivated by a sense of fairness or give-and-take. I believe that he was driven to rack up wins, but he didn't know when or even how to stop. Finally, at the eleventh hour, a solution was reached: I would hold Brian harmless in the event that my parents pursued repayment of the loan.

Brian was to bring the boys to his home in Connecticut every weekend, and if he chose, he could see them in New York on Wednesdays. I had been so eager to get the thing done and official that I offered to drive to a point midway between our homes for the midweek visit. Knowing the limits of my ability to rationally think through every aspect of the agreement, I would discuss proposed changes with friends. They gave me hell about the Wednesday drive.

"What are you thinking?" Carol, a friend and neighbor, asked. "The children will be exhausted by another trip midweek. They'll have homework, playdates, after-school things. The boys will be tied up because of this, and you will be miserable. If he wants to see the children during the week, he can come to New York to see them."

Lisa, my friend since college who had no children, flatly dismissed the plan. "You are still giving up yourself to appease Brian," she pointed out.

It was true; Lisa knew me well. I had always been reluctant to confront Brian, but I had no choice in this instance. I told him that I had made a mistake in offering the midweek trip, that it would not be healthy for the children, and he agreed. Later, I realized that when I was calm and sure of myself (usually an act) and contained the roar in my gut, he would back down. But I hated the process of putting forth my beliefs, my convictions, arguing their truth to Brian. I think I preferred to see myself as wrong because then, in some warped way, I could still see him as in charge, keeping us safe. But safe was the last thing we had been with Brian.

CHAPTER 21

A NEW BEGINNING IN NEW YORK
(2000)

Each Friday afternoon in New York, I left the car at the curb in front of the boys' school on the Upper West Side and rushed to the entrance on Seventy-Ninth Street. There, the children tumbled out, shrugging off school as if it were a vise, feet barely making purchase with the ground. It was there that I had met and been befriended by a few of the other mothers. Most special to me was Nancy. The first time I saw her, I was on the way to pick up the boys at school and we began to chat. Nancy was tall, with curly hair and a powerful stride. She seemed to embody the spirit of the Manhattan woman, more precisely the artistic, bohemian-leaning Upper West Side woman. A prolific writer of children's books, she spoke with authority about everything New York. Initially I was intimidated by her self-confidence, but as we grew closer, we came clean about our fears, the mundane and the serious, and guided each other through the crises that followed.

Nancy's husband, Danny, was a musician and teacher, often reminding me of the stereotypical absent-minded professor. The couple were grown-up hippies, and their two children were the same ages as Noah and Cal. Nancy's daughter was in Noah's class for a few years, and though Ali was only a little less tough than Nancy, Noah felt she needed protection and often took on the role, and when she announced that she was going to play baseball at summer camp he insisted Ali take his soft and worn baseball glove with her. And years later, Nancy would help me stay upright when the unthinkable happened.

After school on Friday, the boys and I would drive north to the meeting spot halfway between Brian's new home in West Hartford and ours in Manhattan. Traveling two hundred and fifty miles every weekend did not bother me. I had dates, friends to see, miles to walk through the city I was rediscovering. I had my life again. I was with my boys and had energy to spare.

Brian married again shortly after we divorced, but this marriage, his third, lasted less than two years. I wondered sometimes if they divorced because he had hit her. Brian once told me that he and his first wife used to have "physical fights." It never crossed my mind that he had abused her. After we separated, I wondered whether "physical fights" was a euphemism for something more one-sided, allowing Brian to believe that his violence was a mutual thing.

The thoughts were transitory and no match for the much stronger belief I had—and still have—that I was the only wife he had hit. That belief, born of a kind of a self-betrayal, is the essence of my Holocaust thinking, but I still can't shake it. A decade later, I learned that Brian had told the boys that we'd also had "physical fights."

Brian blamed me for the demise of his new marriage because, he said, I was intrusively worried about the children when they were in his care. He was right. I would question him every week about what they had eaten, how they dressed, whether they were supervised in a swimming pool, whether they had worn helmets while skiing. Brian could, without skipping a beat, rationalize not feeding the children, not buttoning their coats in the winter, not keeping them in his sight. Knowing how the level of Brian's care could slide in the face of a diversion, I could feel unglued when the boys were with him, and nightmares colonized my sleep.

Sometimes, during the first couple of years after the divorce when the boys were visiting Brian in Connecticut, I would wake in the middle of the night sweating, without even a perfunctory awareness of *anything*. As if I had just been born and every aspect of life, the world I inhabited, was unknown. Yet in those moments, my semiconscious awareness was that I was a mother and I had to find my children. My jackhammering heart rate slowed only when my other senses began to awaken and function. But before that moment came, I catapulted from my bed to the boys' room searching for them in vain. For a few seconds, before I could access the part of my brain that knew Noah and Cal were with Brian, I circled the room like a rabid animal.

When the episode was over and I was back in my own bed, I could not fathom how my heart could withstand such pounding. I'd had nightmares since I was a teenager; I would dream that I was sealed in a coffin-like box and I would wake up screaming. My roommates reported the screams; I never heard them myself.

As time went on, I learned to resist my fears when the boys were with their father. But I believed that if I harassed him enough about the boys' well-being, Brian would be far more careful than if I held my tongue. I didn't care what he thought of me, as long as the boys came back to me whole.

During the week, the three of us lived snug in our apartment in Manhattan, refashioning our lives. Soon we were joined by Chloe, a golden retriever puppy. At night, Noah would insist I lie next to him in the bed that was set perpendicular to Cal's and tell them stories. Sometimes I told the ones my dad had regaled me and my brother with. A favorite was the misadventures of two sparrows, Becky and Sicky, and their friend Georgie, who was a little boy. The three of them were always getting into trouble, invariably because of some ineptitude on Sicky's part. Sicky was a whiner, always coming down with colds and mysterious illnesses. Becky was the beleaguered brains of the operation and had to watch out for Sicky as well as Georgie because Georgie too, had his share of problems.

At six, Cal was a comedian in the tradition of the slapstick borscht-belt greats and performed for us before bedtime. Cal would punctuate his one-liners by jumping up and down on his bed. At the end, if he could, he would fart and then ask, "Did you like the show?" This finale always knocked us out, and sometimes we fell to the floor tangled up and laughing.

CHAPTER 22

A MEETING
(2001-2002)

Our transition to New York was successful, and we were happy with our new lives. The boys liked school, I enjoyed selling real estate, and we had the luxury of living a block from the Metropolitan Museum of Art. We could pop in after school to see a new exhibition of drawings by Leonardo da Vinci or just sit and look at one painting for a while. Grant Wood's *Midnight Ride of Paul Revere* was Cal's favorite. Two years had passed since we left Connecticut.

The terrorist attacks of September 11 came like a gunshot into our center and destroyed any remaining innocence Noah and Cal still possessed after the divorce. That morning, beneath the bluest sky I had ever seen, I heard the news of the first plane hitting the North Tower of the World Trade Center and bolted from my office to the boys' school a few blocks away. Nancy and I sat for hours on the front steps with other parents, waiting, as the children were briefed by their teachers inside the building. A truck packed with firefighters from the fire station down the street sped by in a blare of sirens and we waved to them. Most of the men on that truck died an hour later.

A month after the Towers fell, the city was still heavy with mourning, and each night the decaying humanity-infused ash was brought by the wind into our windows uptown. Each day the lives that had been lost were documented in the newspaper. The faces were uplifted in grins, with unlined skin: they were so young.

The following year, my childhood friend Jo was visiting from San Francisco in the early fall. She traveled to New York every few years to see her parents and old friends. She liked my boys, took pleasure in their low humor, and thought of them as playmates. Jo was their very own Auntie Mame, and she told them pumped-up tales about the trouble we had caused as kids until they held their stomachs in fits of horrified laughter.

The Sunday I was to meet him, Jo was looking after Noah and Cal at our apartment. It was seven in the evening and the restaurant, a bistro with large picture windows framed in red lacquer, was packed. Inside were mostly singles and couples in their twenties and thirties, an occasional family celebrating at a round table. The bar was stacked two and three deep, with young people circling around and leaning into the occupied stools. The sounds of breathing and eating and laughing animated the place with a low, steady roar.

I had arrived early and was uncharacteristically nervous. In the three years since my divorce and the move back to New York, I'd had many dates, most only engaging my desire for dinner, leaving my appetites for intellectual stimulation and human connection unsatisfied. But I enjoyed meeting people and I was always hopeful.

He and I had spoken on the phone two days before, and I was taken by his voice, which was soft and mellifluous. He did not rush his words the way many New Yorkers tended to do, as if mimicking the city's pace. I had the impression that he rose from his desk as we talked, that he was eager. He had found me on a Jewish dating website. He did not have a photo on his profile, but what he had written galvanized me. His words and observations were tough and funny, and I laughed aloud as I read. His use of language cut to the heart; it was farcical, unique, elegant. He wrote of his greatest loves: his daughters and his dog.

I did not care what he looked like; I knew that I had to meet this man. After we agreed to meet, he sent me a photograph; it had been taken from a distance against a mountainous backdrop.

It was hard to move in the cramped space where I stood, but I turned to face the entrance and watched as he came through the door, his eyes tracking the perimeter of the room. They settled on me, and relief moved over his face. As Ron approached, his smile made something inside of me unclasp, and I remembered him.

While much of the memory of that decade-old afternoon in Maine had faded, bright bits of color remained in my mind's eye. Fragmented images like cut glass began to surface. As I watched him maneuver through the crowd's press, it was not so much the memory of the event that stirred me but the intensity of the feelings that had surged then and again now. It was his smile, his dark hair, his prominent chin, and then the slight scent of bergamot when he leaned down to kiss my cheek, that transported me back to the hotel dining room in Maine.

Without context, like an outline in the sand suddenly come to life, he was here again. I was mesmerized and could not look away from his face. Surrounded by moving bodies, it was as if we were in an ellipse of our own. And with the air between us serving as the gentlest of conduits, our cells sought out their counterparts in the other. The connection was made and the enchantment complete.

We studied each other across the small table. There was so much to observe in Ron's face. His prominent features bent this way and that for emphasis or were suddenly static, also for emphasis but of a different kind. His mischievous eyes flashed like a kid's, and his high cheekbones lifted the corners of his mouth when he spoke. His grin was teasing, and I loved it immediately. It was the only thing about him that seemed just a little dangerous.

He talked about his two daughters, the marrow of his life. The older one, Camille, was a figure skater, an introvert, and a beauty. And the little one, Lea, was a devil, a whiz kid, a street-performing magician, and a future polymath.

In just a few moments of conversation, we found that we shared a devotion to Israel; both of us had lived there in the early 1970s. At seventeen, I had studied in Tel Aviv during my family's own Aliyah in 1972—our short-lived immigration to Israel. Ron had studied in Jerusalem during his junior year in college and then returned to Israel two years later as a doctoral student in rhetoric. During the second trip he had met and married his wife, who had fled Casablanca when the climate in Morocco turned against the Jews. Though we had both returned to the United States, our love for Israel had stayed alive through its many governments and cultural and demographic changes. We were curious about the lives we would have lived had we remained in Israel, but oddly, neither of us had felt a pressing desire to return.

He told me stories about his childhood on Mississippi's Gulf Coast. His beginnings were etched there on the sands of the twenty-six miles of the gulf's beaches. Twenty-six miles of pristine sand forbidden to Blacks during the scorching summers prior to the late 1960s. While many of the characteristics of Ron's Southern upbringing would eventually become foreign, even repulsive, their place in his psyche was fixed.

His youth had been an acidic mix of joy and disgust. His first intimation that something was rotten in his affable Southern hometown had come when he was six.

Shushing his protests, Ron's babysitter Belle set him down in a seat at the front of the bus. His eyes followed her journey gripping one hanging strap after another as she moved to the back. As Ron grew older, the horrors perpetrated in his town in the name of racial purity became a monster he could not fight, and he began to plan his escape. Ron's disgust eased somewhat when civil rights legislation was finally forced down the throats of the segregationists, bringing them to their white-robed knees. But the Klan, which his father had taught him to despise, was not neutralized but continued to function in shadow.

Ron's father, Zeke, an air force mechanic who had served in Wales during World War II, had been nearly wrecked by dispatching Allied pilots into German and French skies, knowing that most of them would not return. They were young men with little fear or inhibition of war who in the heat of battle forgot their mothers' faces until the mission went wrong and they reached for her in their final seconds of helpless grief.

Passing through New Orleans in the adrenaline-filled morning of the war's end, Zeke met the incandescent eighteen-year-old Elaine Rubenstein on a train traveling south from New Jersey. After pursuing and marrying Elaine, Zeke quickly established himself in the textile trade of Meridian, Mississippi. A northerner and an independent thinker, he had difficulty adhering to the segregation rules of the day. The sheriff, visiting his store, patiently explained the difficulty Zeke would encounter staying in business if he allowed Black women to sit at the counter alongside the White women and thumb through the Vogue dress patterns. Zeke's solution was to get rid of the stools. Somehow it was more acceptable for the women, Black and White, to stand at the counter together.

To his wife's family—a rowdy, closely tied bunch, the sort of Jews who broke the Yom Kippur fast with hot dogs midday at the Waffle House—Zeke was an oddity, one they accepted with cautious affection. After all, despite multiple business failures, he provided Elaine with a new Pontiac Bonneville every three years, a golf membership at Gulfport's modest country club, and three handsome sons.

Ron's own brand of Zionism might never have surfaced had he and his family not been such stark oddities in Gulfport, where the only synagogue—small in membership and served only by itinerant rabbis—had been established by Ron's great-grandmother. But it worked well enough, and the three brothers' Jewish education was supplemented by the much-anticipated visits from United Jewish Appeal fundraisers who drank whiskey sours in the living room.

Pushing through the UJA ranks, Zeke eventually became an impassioned speaker for the new state of Israel. He may have found himself in Mississippi, but Zeke would be damned if his three boys were going to grow up as Southerners.

Ron left as soon as he could after finishing high school, called by his older brother Hillary who had already made his escape to California and was a student at Berkeley. With some effort, Ron was able to shake off the stench of segregation but held on to the memories of the moss-hung oak trees and the lantana flower, whose scent and hues of pink, yellow, and orange could hurtle him back home.

On the surface, Ron's story seems different from mine, but underneath, at its heart, it was the same. A furnace burned there, a fire fed like mine by the Holocaust. Israel, the place created from the detritus of the Jews massacred in Europe, pressed its weight on us. It was a spiritual detritus that haunted the sleep of the survivors. For the ones who had survived, the cries of their murdered loved ones became alarms that rang unsilenced throughout the landscape of the Holocaust's aftermath until the short man with the wild white hair declared the establishment of the state of Israel and became her first prime minister.

This ancient soil might well have been the sanctuary of the six million murdered Jews had Israel come into being a decade earlier. Yet, the new country could hardly become their final resting place, for how could the souls of the martyred find their way across the sea to a homeland that had been only a desperate fever dream of Europe's Zionists? But for the victims of the Final Solution, there was someone who survived, someone who still remembered a smile, a laugh, a child's favorite lullaby. And in this way, the vanished were carried in hand and heart to the promised land.

CHAPTER 23

THE WORLD FILLS WITH COLOR
(2002-2003)

O n my second date with Ron, Jo met us after dinner for a
drink. At a table in the dark clubby bar of an elegant but
soon-to-be-demolished hotel (shortly to be replaced by
multi-million-dollar apartments), I studied Ron's profile as he
leaned back in his chair, hands pushed deep in the pockets of
his pleated wool pants. He worked hard to charm Jo and was
successful, and I was excited. Since my divorce, I had not had
a date that had lasted more than two hours. This one lasted six.
Jo, ever cautious, said he seemed like a good guy.

Our first night together was in Ron's apartment, which was
above his office. After his divorce, he had bought the five-unit
red brick building across the street from the fire station. The
century-old structure was situated in a Victorian village built
originally as an artist colony and summer retreat on the Long
Island Sound. The apartment Ron took for himself was the one
that commanded the lowest rent.

The night was moonless and silent; the only light enter-
ing the room came from the street lamp in front of the fire
station. We had been dating nearly two months, but this

was my first time in Ron's home. He brought a bottle of scotch into the bedroom and set it with two small glasses on a wooden table next to the bed. In my memory, the table was rickety and may have been a repurposed fruit crate. Ron showed me how to drink the amber peat liquid, to keep it on my tongue for a few seconds before letting it go down my throat slowly. Then he kissed me. And again, until it was time to drink once more.

I woke some hours later, thinking that the fire station alarm had sounded, but I might have dreamed it, the night stretching long and dense, the scotch messing with my dreams and sleep coming and going. All while I remained within the circumference of his arms.

Shivering from the release of years of neglected emotions, I looked out through the window at the streetlight's beam. Electrons falling from one energy level to the one below it emitted photons of electricity, creating the light that I was now fixed upon. It seemed that the light was a map of what lay ahead, a thing so encompassing that I could not turn away or run from it. I knew it was a way back to myself.

The sleep I had with Ron was a revelation. I had not shared a bed since the separation four years earlier, and I felt vulnerable. What if I had a nightmare and screamed? But with the first touch, my fears fell away and I folded into him. When it seemed that we had to sleep, at least for a while, Ron arranged us so that my back was tucked into his chest. He lay on his side behind me this way, his hands snaking under my arms, over my ribs, ending in a fan across my stomach, my knees nearly touching his fingertips. It was the deep sleep of childhood nights between my grandparents in their bed. I use the analogy still. With Ron I felt cloaked in the safety, peace, and nobility of my grandparents' love.

From the beginning, we understood that we would be together, and we began the complicated and difficult business of merging our lives. There was dissent from nearly every corner, the loudest from my mother who did not trust him or my choices anymore.

Cal watched Ron carefully. He was friendly and asked a lot of questions, but Cal was suspicious of the way he was looking at me. I could imagine what was playing out in his nine-year-old head: "Mom is acting weird. She seems to be fluttering, like a bird or something. Why is she so nervous? Noah doesn't seem to have a problem with this guy. He can be dumb that way sometimes."

"So, guess what, guys?" I said. "Ron is going to take Chloe to his house for a couple of days so she can spend some time with his puppy, Dolce."

Cal stopped fiddling with the LEGO in his hands and looked up at me. Had I lost my mind?

"Why?" he asked.

Ron answered, "Your mom works hard, and this will give her a little break."

"Mom doesn't need a break. She's fine."

"Chloe will be back home this weekend. It will be fun for her, don't you think?"

"No."

"Cal." I gave him the look he knew preceded my getting mad. He didn't say anything more.

Later, after Ron and Chloe left, Cal asked, "Why is he taking our dog? What if he doesn't give her back?"

Is that possible? I thought. I barely knew him; what if I was jumping into something bad again? I knew the answer but could not articulate it to Cal. I would be with Ron for the rest of my life.

Ron wrote me love emails every day. "Six weeks ago, I didn't know you existed and now you inhabit me."

The first time he told me he loved me, he had used a bar of soap to draw the words in a heart pierced by an arrow on my bathroom mirror. When we first began to spend our nights together, Ron woke me by speaking into the back of my neck. "Will you marry me? I think we should get married."

"You're crazy. Go back to sleep," I answered.

"But will you marry me?"

After about a week of this, I began to respond differently when he asked the same question. "I will try," I said, but I already knew it was done. We married four months later in the spring, between my birthday and his. As it had been when Jo and I met, I had little conscious thought about the connection while it was being made. It just was, and the only question might have been about the adequacy of life before.

There is a thing that happens with Ron that I still cannot put my finger on. When I look at him, I feel a lifting. I slide into the space around him, with him, and there is a magnetic grab that locks me into place. I am not a solitary being any longer. I am part of him but in no way diminished. I am more than I was the moment before, heightened and fuller. I feel a completeness, a circularity that I hadn't known before—all in barely a second. I am accustomed to it now and notice it only occasionally, but in the beginning, it was a disturbing crash of charged atoms.

CHAPTER 24

I MARRY AGAIN
(2003)

The speed at which our lives melded together might have seemed to some like an alarming wave. The situation was exacerbated by the troublemaking grandiosity of our feelings, which made us impulsive and sometimes thoughtless. When we announced our intention to marry, barely two months after our first date, our families had been suspicious and apprehensive. Friends, parents, brothers all asked, "Are you *sure* that you are sure?"

My mother did an Internet background check on Ron. "It's so fast!" she said. "Why not just wait a little bit? Just live together. You don't need a piece of paper at this stage in your life!"

"Mom, that doesn't feel right to us, and it wouldn't be good for the children."

"Do you know the statistics on the survival of second marriages with children? You have a better chance of being hit by lightning!"

I brought Ron to meet my ninety-eight-year-old grandmother Rose at her assisted living apartment in a leafy section of Queens. In his attempt to ingratiate himself to her, Ron found himself in more challenging waters than he had encountered with Jo a few weeks earlier.

Finally, after some bland chitchat, my grandmother, with a skeptical look in her eyes, said, "You know you're too old to get married. Who needs it anyway?"

I felt warmth suffusing my cheeks.

She said that when she was widowed in her seventies, she had never considered remarrying.

I was insulted. After all, I was still in my forties and started to say so. "But, Nonny, I'm only forty-sev—"

"Aha!" she interrupted, looking at Ron with pity. "Forty? You think she's *forty*?"

I was in shock; my grandmother Rose was trying to sabotage my upcoming marriage. She was actually hoping that she had caught me lying about my age. What a coup to report back to my mother!

Ron sat very still. He was speechless, his face stuck in the smile it had been wearing a moment before.

"Wow," he said when we were in the car driving over the bridge into Manhattan. "Impressive show of loyalty, that was."

"I guess they're not excited about this marriage."

He looked at me sideways. "You think?"

Ugly stories, previously concealed secrets of friends, were suddenly disclosed. Stepchildren were hell and could kill you. Ex-spouses were only marginally less insidious, but in certain cases could be even worse. Rejected and enraged, the sociopathic ex would turn to the nearest, most malleable target, a child. And what a target it was, a wounded child, who might become an unwitting accomplice to the humiliated, tossed-aside ex-spouse.

We heard everything but listened only to ourselves and married four months later when we were still strangers. Except for brief interludes following nasty disagreements we had in our early years, we never regretted our decision.

Our wedding took place on a Thursday afternoon in April at the synagogue affiliated with the school the boys attended. Cal was performing in a school play the same afternoon in the sanctuary. I caught him just before the ceremony while he was in full makeup with mustache and beard. Pulling him into the bathroom, I scrubbed the makeup from his face and then ran up the stairs in new high-heeled shoes to get married. In the rabbi's study, Ron and I stood under the wedding canopy, the *huppah,* and made promises to each other. The children circled us as Ron's brother Hillary and my friend Lisa held up the edges of the canopy.

Later that evening, in my apartment, Ron was elated. He was filled with exhilaration and anticipation of our life together. Unwrapping what he had long held inside, he wept, his tears falling onto my breast. I held him and watched his face open like a flower. I had never seen such joy so near before. That night, Ron had to return home to Long Island so that his daughters would not sleep alone in the house. I was disappointed, but there was no better validation of my decision to marry this man. I saw that he would jump into a lake of fire for his children.

When Ron married me, he married my problems and then my grief. He was bequeathed all the memories of the time we would illogically view as the deferment of a life together after our encounter in Maine. We had come to each other with so much that did not belong in a new marriage. The pain of the past emerged sporadically, at first here and there when the odd thing would trigger it, then with regularity as we became more interlaced. Ron's devotion to those he loved was the light he followed, and thus the facts of my life with Brian ate away at him. There was little relief because we saw Brian twice every weekend when we traveled to Danbury with the boys.

With Brian, I had known with an absolute, but abstract, certainty that no creature should be abused. Yet it was only after marrying Ron that I seriously began to question my long-held sense that I had been as culpable as Brian was in his violence. That the problem lay with me because I possessed an innate defect that had provoked Brian beyond any human ability to maintain control.

During the early part of our marriage, Ron would notice and question my thoughts and behaviors that he found puzzling. He noticed that I often took blame in a knee-jerk fashion, when upon rational thinking, it was obvious that I could not have been at fault. Yet self-recrimination and guilt were familiar, ingrained and what I automatically reverted to, especially in times of stress. These default attitudes and feelings had been an indelible component of my emotional and psychological functioning for as long as I could remember, the bitter remains of my legacy as a child of Holocaust survivors. But to Ron they were new, perplexing, and dysfunctional, and he called them out whenever he saw them in operation. At first when he confronted me with my irrational thinking, I became defensive, but over time, these old beliefs made their way to consciousness and I began to actively dismantle the conviction that I was inherently defective and that a life of guilt was my birthright.

When Ron and I would argue, mostly about the children's interactions or the laxity with which we believed the other parented, I took a mulish pleasure in the knowledge that I could yell at him and say awful things and still there would be no hand coming at me. Without fear of reprisal, fiery aspects of my personality emerged and I was less inhibited about saying exactly what I thought. When I told Ron this, he thought it was perverse but was patient as my thinking straightened itself out.

If our arguments veered toward the intense, we would leave the house and drive around town with the car windows shut, free to shout without concern of being overheard. It was cathartic when we were just beginning the process of learning how to adjust our behavior or habits to accommodate each other. And each disagreement with Ron was an opportunity to understand and make right the historical and skewed thought patterns that had allowed me to accept my life with Brian.

CHAPTER 25

A BLENDING
(2004)

As we burrowed into each other, Ron and I were protective of the life we had begun to build. Our children were tolerant of our obvious delight in each other, but we knew the transition was hard for them.

Looking back at that period, ours was a hollow understanding because we underestimated the extent to which the children might feel real pain. Ron and I had both been divorced for a few years before we met, and following our divorces, our children had received our undivided attention. What was it like for them, still not privy to the ways of adults, to see each of us gazing in adoration at the other—someone who was essentially a stranger? Ron and I often talked about this, especially when one of the children would act out. But we knew that the dividedness they were experiencing could overwhelm us and threaten what we had. It was simply too dangerous to our hard-won joy to acknowledge that we were viewing the children's experience through an illusory lens. We became selfish, refusing to let go of any glint of happiness.

The children tried to grasp this new order as best they could. Lea, at twelve, preferred to be in charge and had a mind that was sharper than her tongue. She seemed to have taken her parents' divorce in stride (Camille had stronger memories of the end of her parents' marriage, having already been a pre-teen at the time) and preferred anything—studying, hanging out with friends, earning quarters with her street-performing magician act—to discussing feelings. Someone (not I) had the idea that Lea should accompany us to choose my engagement ring. Upon arriving at the shop, she promptly picked out a lovely pink sapphire and diamond ring. Then, having completed her self-assigned task, Lea fell to the ground, arms and legs flailing, and wept and railed against our approaching marriage.

Once when she was thirteen, Lea wrote me a letter explaining why I should continue to take her on shopping adventures even when she was angry with me. She wrote, "I like you very much. You are a strong woman, but I don't like who you are when you are with my father." Her perceptions intrigued me and still do because of my history. Was Lea simply expressing her desire to possess both her father and me separately, or did she see something in me that changed when I was with a man? Over the years, our relationship has had incarnations that have wounded us both, but, as Lea insisted during one of our recent hurt-feeling debriefs, "We are family, and you don't get to change that."

Camille's only comment when we told her of our plan to marry was, "Really, so soon?" She had black hair and eyes nearly as dark. I was surprised by her angelic beauty the first time we met. With her rush of black curls, Camille resembled a figure in a Venetian painting. She and her father possessed a shorthand language around the business of skating. They were a working pair, traveling to practices and competitions together. Ron had become skeptical—but remained hopeful—about the world Camille's talent led them to and about her chances to rise above the masses of children who all wanted to be the best.

The pressures and demands of skating grew in direct relation to Camille's success, but they had also provided a respite from the rigors of Ron's marriage. Time was surgically meted out for Camille to skate each day while going to school. Still, Ron was delighted to wake before dawn each morning to drive her to practice at an ice rink that had a low admission fee and was close to a school that was flexible enough to allow Camille to use her skating hours in lieu of mandatory physical education classes.

Camille enjoyed our connection and welcomed my participation in her skating life. She was reserved but had a fiercely protective bent. On our first outing, she broke her silence to gently admonish her father when he insisted that I taste a particular pastry. He would not take no for answer, and I was too nervous to eat. Seeing my discomfort, Camille said, "Papa, she doesn't want it," and with a slight flick of her wrist she moved the fork away from my mouth.

Laughing, we recalled the incident twenty years later when an aggressive employee tried to extort a large tip after Camille's move into her new apartment. As the man edged uncomfortably close to me while complaining about the hundred dollars that I had given him, Camille slipped into warrior mode trying to figure out where the movers had put her baseball bat.

Originally, Ron and I thought that we would retain both of our households to minimize the disruption for everyone. The first spring it had been fun this way. The boys and I would leave early in the morning from Ron's house on Long Island and drive to the city with egg sandwiches that he had made for Noah and Cal, and a small thermos of coffee for me. These trips would be some of our last times alone, just the three of us. We talked about the impact of the marriage on our lives. Our discussions were mixed with plans for dentist and doctor visits and baseball games in Connecticut.

But soon it was clear to everyone how unmanageable it was to commute to New York City nearly every day. In addition, maintaining two households kept our families too separate. Cal was not eager to move because it would mean leaving his school and his friends, but Noah wanted the change. That summer, we moved to Ron's coral-colored Victorian house in Sea Cliff. I thought it was going to be a smooth transition for everyone.

But the transition was not smooth, rocking tectonically with the emotions of each party to the marriage. Four children and two ex-spouses, each with a hurt that was specific to how our union had injured their understanding of the place they held in their family. Everything had changed. I jumped in headfirst, determined to blend two families that might not have connected under different circumstances.

How I wish I had stayed in the background, allowing everyone to adjust at his or her own pace. But my anxiety pushed me to intrude whenever I saw strife among the children—perhaps I tried to fill the hurt spaces caused by misunderstandings, frustrations, or just a simple reluctance to share. Simply living together and learning each other's rhythms might have allowed us to evolve into a cohesive unit over time. Maybe we never would have fit together, although I was unwilling to consider that terrible possibility.

The reality was that the children fit, but each one in his or her own way. The relationships they eventually built had their own fluctuations, times of intense connection and times when barely a word was exchanged for days. Once when I was upset with Cal for doing his homework carelessly, Lea appeared at the top of the stairs, headphones in her ears. Without a word, she took Cal outside and literally stood between him and me so that continuing the argument was impossible. I can still see Cal peeking out from behind her back. I think he was amazed that she got me to stop yelling.

Sometimes the stress of managing the needs of these separate lives—the boys' weekends in Connecticut, Noah's sports teams, Camille's skating responsibilities, Cal's simple desire for everyone's happiness, Lea's ferocious pursuit of academic and social brilliance—peaked and nobody spoke to each other. When this happened, I was despondent, seeing the children's quiet as a disruptive headwind rather than a pause needed solely to recalibrate.

Not having the advantage of biology, I wanted us all to be as close as possible. There is so much I wish I had done differently after I married Ron, but the terrain was unknown, and I felt vulnerable without any familiar touchstones. Our families may have been similar in the broadest of strokes, but there were profound differences grounded in the ways our broods had evolved.

I had no frame of reference and was heedless of the cautions offered by other parents who had married again. I heard the truth in their words, but in a peripheral way that I could easily ignore. They spoke of huge challenges, but I dismissed their concerns as cynical advice from tired parents who had abandoned any hope of creating harmony within a blended family. They had been disappointed, but I was immune to their malady. Despite our inadequacies, our intentions were good, so the outcome had to be good.

CHAPTER 26

EXPLORING THE NEW WORLD
(2005)

After we married, Ron and I lived on a learning curve and continued to find that our interests, ideas, and values were fundamentally similar, with only occasional areas of discord. Although the thousands of specific traits and attributes we each possessed would reveal themselves gradually in the years ahead, our core aspects were clearly visible from the beginning and made our experience of each other visceral and complex. I believe that this clarity came from an underlying connectedness, the same connection that had communicated itself in the seconds of our meeting in the hotel dining room in Kennebunkport. Our hasty marriage, almost impossible to explain to others, was its consequence.

It was as if we were sleepwalking toward each other. Although we had not realized how much our parts overlapped, a commonality that stood out quickly was our love of travel, especially to Europe. My passion for all things European came partly from my European-born parents and also because aspects of the day-to-day life there, its earthiness, and the mindset of its citizens resonated with me. At seventeen,

I had taken my first solo trip to Amsterdam and Germany, thrilled to be traveling on Europe's rail system. I experienced strange feelings, hard to decipher, when I met older Germans. My reactions were difficult to process, so I would swallow my fears and look away.

When Ron and I visited Europe together for the first time, we sought out places that most fluently expressed a country's artistic and emotional character. We were fascinated by the people we saw on the street, their absolute otherness: how they lived each day, what they ate, how they dressed with loose scarves flowing from their necks (Ron was thrilled to see the greens and golds and reds of the elegant trousers and sport coats men wore while zipping around on their Vespas), the books they held, the political and philosophical ideas that seemed to be absorbed like air. We spent our days walking, talking with strangers, and sitting at cafés watching life stream by.

Ron had been abroad many times yet had resisted any opportunity to visit Italy. He told me this with a meaningful look in the weeks before our engagement. He said that he would travel to Italy only with his truest love, and this became a euphemism for marriage. The theater of his mind danced with images of lovers against a backdrop of ancient Roman aqueducts and the frescoes of Michelangelo and Raphael. We spent our honeymoon there.

Our life appeared charmed, and we were grateful for our gifts of time, means, and strength of body. When we were in Italy, we walked or biked for hours each day. We drank red wine from barrels and ate pasta in trattorias in ancient, asymmetrically shaped stone buildings from which laundry hung to dry on rope strung over stone streets. Sometimes, drowsy from a wine-saturated feast, we would nap like hobos on the grass of a nearby park.

Once, I forgot my bicycle helmet at a restaurant in a tiny village overlooking the city of Florence. It had been a hard ride uphill to the place, and after lunch we already had ridden a few kilometers back toward Florence when I remembered the helmet. I started to turn my bike around to retrieve it, but Ron, looking at me strangely over his shoulder, had already started riding back up the hill to the restaurant. I stretched out on a bench in the sun, my hands around the back of my head as a breeze moved deliciously over me filling my chest like cotton candy. Each such act by Ron was a disruption to an order that had been built in my childhood and played out in my relationship with Brian. Although I was still untangling all of this, I took great pleasure in its fall.

We traveled to the south of France, and when the euro and the dollar were nearly equal in value we bought an apartment in a nineteenth-century building. Small by American standards with two tiny bedrooms, it had glass doors opening from the rooms to a narrow terrace that spanned the length of the apartment. The terrace looked out on a walking street lined on both sides with historic stucco buildings with slate roofs.

From the street below, I would whistle for Ron, and if he was inside, he would come to the iron railing and smile down at me. We would banter back and forth for a few minutes, amused by the funny looks we would get from the pedestrians. Then we would decide on a plan for the next hours, which would involve eating, food shopping, walking north into the hills, or biking east to the cellophane-blue water of Cap d'Antibes for a swim.

At night, we ate our dinner on the terrace looking toward the medieval part of town with its enormous clock tower lighting up the surrounding streets. Low clouds floated over the red-tiled rooftops, which at twilight were circled by parakeets calling to each other before settling down for the night. Dusk fell late in Cannes when the sky exploded in shades of indigo and cobalt that darkened to ink.

Cannes was in love with blue. There were blue-and-white motifs of life at sea in the ubiquitous striped boater shirts worn by fashionistas and the men who worked on yachts. Mothers wore delicate robin's-egg blue-and-white sundresses, their daughters in complementing pinafores. They promenaded and held the hands of their *grands-mères,* who were barely dressed in clinging slip dresses in beige or cream with lace at the décolletage like lingerie. The grandmothers had skinny bronzed chests and bird-like legs that must have been grateful to support only tiny bodies fed mostly by cigarettes. They walked the fabulous streets with baskets, narrow shopping carts, and expensive-logoed totes, stopping at the morning open-air market to purchase fruits and vegetables and cheese before visiting their favorite butcher.

Somehow, we had reaped something magical in the year we had been married, and we wanted to bring the children to France the following summer. I was thrilled at the prospect, but Brian complained to Noah that taking a two-week break from baseball practice could destroy his major-league dreams. Immediately, any possible anticipatory pleasure Noah might have relished was gone. I had been so excited to bring my boys to this beautiful place, but Noah was wedged tightly between my hopes for him and the baseball dreams of his father. As the years passed, I could feel more and more of Noah's anguish from this conflict.

My parents accompanied us on that trip, and the boys took turns staying with them at the little hotel near our apartment. Noah seemed freer when he was with his grandparents, his conflicts scattering in the warm breezes. There wasn't room enough for both boys to sleep in the hotel room with my parents, so Noah was with them the most. Although they were supposed to take turns, Noah would incentivize Cal by giving him a few euros. For Noah, at nearly fourteen years old, there was still no better place for him than with his Nana and Papa.

I should have spent more time alone with Noah that summer, talking, swimming, being, but I thought we had all the time in the world. Even now, I focus on what I did not do, the distance between the mother I was and my idea of maternal perfection. It's impossible to achieve that state, yet it is still more natural to blame myself. As if, had I just done some things differently, all of Brian's violence would have remained in check.

CHAPTER 27

NOAH LEAVES
(2005-2009)

Shortly after Noah started high school, he announced that he wanted to live with his father in Connecticut; Cal followed his brother's lead. I was shocked and dug in my heels; I could not imagine turning the boys over to their father.

There were loud, painful arguments. We argued about Noah's grades, time spent on his sports, Ron's treatment of him, and most agonizing, his behavior toward me, which had begun to veer into a disdain that I felt had its roots in the attitudes of his father. Noah wanted to be in Connecticut where he could play as much baseball as possible, with constant access to practice fields. I felt that Brian put baseball first, and while that was enticing, Noah also wanted to be away from our new family.

Noah's relationship with Ron had disintegrated; Ron was increasingly impatient with Noah, confronting the boys when they misbehaved. It was anathema to him if my children did not show me complete respect. In fairness, there had been a looseness to the way I had raised them that Ron took issue with. He believed that boys were more difficult than girls, a holdover from struggles with his own father who had demanded a great deal from his sons, yet disappointed them constantly. I thought that structure and routine were important but not necessarily crucial—that with enough love and understanding, children would be respectful of the world but never fearful of its possibilities. My parents and friends told me that sometimes the boys were unruly and rude to me, but I never doubted my sons' intrinsic love.

Noah and Cal had witnessed their father verbally lash out at me. Brian mocked my parenting directly to me and, I later learned, to the boys when he was alone with them. When Noah was ten, he broke his wrist and needed to take a few weeks off from soccer. When I gave Brian the doctor's instructions the following weekend, he exploded, and the three of us stood silent as he yelled, insisting that a break from soccer was ridiculous. I rarely raised my voice to Brian in front of the boys except for one painful occasion, and they knew that their father felt free to say whatever he wanted to me. I felt that when they saw Brian's willingness to bash me in their presence, they began to confuse fear with respect.

One Friday, we brought the boys to meet their father and waited in the parking lot of Starbucks as Noah and Cal collected their things from our car. Brian was angry because I had said I would curtail Noah's sports if his grades slipped. He was taken off guard, seeming to forget that Ron was standing with Dolce in the grass a few yards away, and he started to scream. He poked his finger into my chest to make his point.

And then I lost it, shouting back at him, "What are you going to do, Brian? Hit me like you did when we were married?"

I saw the words leave my mouth and hover in front of the boys' frozen faces. I wanted to reach out to pull them back before they could be heard. Cal and Noah had never witnessed the physical abuse; this I believed. Now they knew, and they were too young to know! Knowing about it would be the end of their childhood.

I heard Brian say to Ron, "It's not true, Ron. You know how she is."

Ron turned away and climbed into the driver's seat. "The lying bastard," Ron muttered as we pulled out of the parking lot.

Around the time Noah started to talk about leaving, he began to have pain in his shoulder and elbow. I brought him to an orthopedist who treated professional hockey players. After he examined Noah, the doctor—restrained and all-business—explained that a boy of Noah's age could not play baseball more than two seasons a year because he risked permanent damage to his arm and shoulder. He described the delicacy and vulnerability of growth plates. Brian had Noah on a year-round hitting and throwing schedule; it did not change after the doctor's visit.

The mood at home became onerous as Noah and I continued to clash. He grew quiet, aloof. I felt him disengaging from me, from our life together, almost as though he had a mission and I was standing in his way. Ron and Cal tried to stay to the side, but both were drawn in as Noah was adamant that he and Cal were both leaving.

Cal stolidly weathered the challenges at home, focusing on the books that he read with more than his usual eagerness. The conflicts between me and Noah agonized him. Cal had always craved quiet acceptance and love from us and, crucially, the freedom to follow his inner voice in peace.

Then, Brian sued me for custody of the boys in Connecticut, and at the same time, I brought an action against him for custodial interference in New York. Brian claimed in his suit that I was abusive. Incidents where I attempted to discipline or guide Noah were transformed by Brian into ugly encounters showing me to be incapable of parenting. The irony of his accusations in view of what I had received from Brian's fists and feet was lost on no one, and the process of defending myself was excruciating.

We suffered through a visit from a social worker investigating Brian's claims. It was humiliating, and I felt that I was being punished for the times I had contacted child protective services as a social worker. But the woman who came to our home was kind and listened as we described events of the previous months: I in tears, Ron stoic. She told us to try not to worry and to continue as we had, that the case would be closed as unfounded. It was, and we did not hear from her again.

For years, I viewed this experience as a stain on my character and devastatingly, my mothering, for after all wasn't it only the worst, most-lacking parents who received such a visit? Now I know it for what it was: Brian's need to fabricate a case against me that would portray him as the boys' rescuer. And perhaps in doing so he could upend history and make me the abuser.

Brian's suit prevailed over the one I had filed in New York, and we landed in Connecticut's family court. He told the children they must vilify me as a mother, and in their conflict, neither of my boys could extricate themselves from their father's demands.

But within two months, Brian and I had hammered out an agreement that I thought I could live with. Cal would live at his father's home during the week, and every Friday through Sunday he would be with me in New York. Noah, at fourteen, would decide on his own when or if he chose to see me. Never insecure about my love, Cal went with his brother and his father when they said he must. He spoke later about the things his father told him to say about me, things that were not true. This haunts him still, no matter how much we tell him that at only twelve years old, he had been put in an agonizing and untenable position.

Before the agreement was finalized, I made an unusual demand. In exchange for my agreeing to the change in physical custody, Brian would enter treatment with the psychologist to whom he had acknowledged beating me. My thinking was that if Brian could speak without fear about what he had done, he might explore his violent tendencies and learn what drove his rage. Then, I believed, he would be far less likely to pass on his behavior to the children. I was terrified that in his home the boys would emulate or become victims of Brian's violence.

The judge admonished Brian not to keep the children away from me, a ludicrous possibility I had never considered. "Don't you dare do anything to keep these boys away from their mother!"

Across the courtroom's aisle, Brian sat with his attorney. He nodded his head in vehement assent like a bobble head doll. The words of the judge were prescient, though they meant little to me at the time. I thought my relationship with Noah was inviolable. But Brian did keep him from me, a carefully thought-out campaign that, in my absolute certainty of Noah's love, I could not have foreseen.

Now that the original custody plan had been turned on its head, I realized I would no longer be the school parent and all that came with it. Despite the turmoil brought on by these radical changes, the idea of being with Cal during his free time was exhilarating in an almost forbidden way, as if we were both going to play hooky. Brian and I continued to have joint legal custody, which was a relief because it kept us equal under the law and meant that Brian's efforts to keep Cal away from me would be curtailed by the court. His intentions toward me were not good, and his aim was to wound.

We continued to battle in court for four years. Documents, briefs, and motions piled up, and our heavy, spilling file became a focus of derision in the family court. The years there felt a lifetime long and elastic, the time stretching and contracting and overlapping. Days were spent in corridors waiting to enter the courtroom or sitting in the courtroom sick to my stomach as I anticipated the judge's decision. Everything always seemed as if it were happening at once. It was the emotional equivalent of a building collapsing leisurely on top of me.

Although the beginning was like a seismic wave gutting everything in its path, we soon adapted to the new routine. During the four-year custody struggle, court dates were battles and meetings with lawyers and therapists were the strategy sessions. The psychological evaluations and reunification therapy that came later were meant to be our reconstruction. And there was the constant inner gnawing as I realized that Noah was leaving me. Everybody told me it wasn't so, but I knew.

Cal was torn, but Noah, shielded by his certainty and alignment with his father, developed a singular rage toward me. My father would say that he was comforted by the knowledge that Noah was so sure of everything—who was good, who was bad. That any ambivalence might have been torture for Noah because of how he was built. My father believed what he said, though its truth deprived him of his beloved boy.

The court was frustrated and impatient with us, angry at the many lawyers I brought—three in four years. They resented the fact that I would not stop, that I kept coming back to Connecticut demanding my sons, that I wasted their time with briefs and motions, which they never seemed to read. They hated the thickness of our custody case file, holding it up in disgust as proof of the vileness of the proceedings.

I was driven to keep fighting because I believed that continuing on was the only way I could stem Brian's alienating behavior and limit its infection of Cal. How might the outcome have differed had I stopped?

In retrospect, the custody fight was wretched and unproductive, and Brian cemented Noah's alienation by using my actions in court as evidence that I was bad and Brian himself was the victim. But had I not been so single-minded, would Brian have succeeded in keeping Cal from me as well? Brian had aimed his alienating behavior at Cal relentlessly, perhaps because of his son's loyalty to me, but Cal resisted. His engagement with his own interior world was his refuge and acted as a protective buffer.

Noah, I believed, wanted to make his father proud and was more vulnerable to Brian's manipulations. And I had been rigidly on the defense and too frightened of what it all meant to understand and help my son. I do not need to analyze the guilt I still feel for allowing Noah to navigate this terrible time on his own.

While dealing with the motions I brought, the court was alert and Brian did not try to prevent Cal from coming to New York. But it was a pyrrhic victory that had me in knots because Noah's anger increased in direct proportion to Brian's. Noah tried so hard to shoulder some of the emotional blowback to give his father relief, to protect him.

A year later, the therapist tasked by the court to help reunify us said that Brian was evil because he had used his psychological skills on his children. He said that Brian would never rest until he saw me living in a tiny apartment above a storefront. The image was vivid and stuck with me, eventually transforming into a tiny but romantic Paris attic apartment where, like Ernest Hemingway, I would spend my days writing.

Each court date, Ron drove while I tried to fortify myself for what lay ahead. He would sit very straight in his suit in the back of the courtroom, my bodyguard. When I became exhausted, I faltered and wanted to give up, but Ron lifted me as my father had and spun me around until we dropped gratefully into the comfortable seats of a plane headed to Europe. As we plowed through the legal morass, we also hiked the hills of Cinque Terre, biked the Alpes-Maritimes, wandered the mysterious streets of Venice in winter, and watched our breath steam in the wet heat of New Delhi. Once again, Ron saved me, and during our fifth year of marriage I began to trust that he always would.

Noah did not change his mind about coming to New York, and the court allowed him to decide when we would see each other. I was distraught and felt increasingly unhinged as he refused my calls and would not speak to my parents. It was like a death for them and was the only time in my life that I saw my father depressed. My kind, brilliant, and funny dad had been toppled. I tried to explain to my parents what was happening, what parental alienation meant, but they could not sift through the psychological hyperbole to fathom what they had done to cause Noah to turn away from them.

Brian's campaign to alienate Noah from me and my family had begun in earnest immediately after the boys moved to Connecticut, but the idea had likely been conceived after the divorce. Now the message was no longer just insinuated. I, along with anyone and anything connected to me or the family in New York, was bad, and Brian was good. A narrative was spun and mushroomed before I noticed it gaining heft.

I was usually a few steps behind Brian, and the defensive position was my default mode. But Ron consistently tried to envision Brian's next move and plan a response. I had been told that Brian's narrative seemed to aim to obliterate me as mother in Noah's mind. I was the evil parent whom Noah should not see, and it was a just a matter of time before Cal would follow.

At first, I did not imagine there could be any permanence to this. How could it possibly stick? How could Noah reject me? I, who had slept on the floor next to Noah's bed whenever he'd been sick, was to be thrown away? And Brian, who had slammed the bedroom door to block out the noise as I carried Noah to the bathroom to vomit, was the one who was adored.

I was overwhelmed with feelings that roared through me, disrupting any psychological equilibrium I might have possessed. Nothing made sense, and I blamed Brian completely. I was hit by what I believed to be his malevolent goal: to annihilate me as he himself might have felt when I left him. What more searing way to do this than to have Noah remove me from his heart?

The therapy Brian was to have had underpinned my consent for the boys to move to Connecticut. But the therapy never happened. Brian told the court that the psychologist that knew of Brian's violence would not accept his insurance, and in any case his and the doctor's schedules did not mesh. The court refused to compel Brian to see Dr. Reid and allowed him to find his own therapist—someone to whom Brian could tell any story that he wished. I always had trouble feeling my anger toward Brian and usually attached it to those I saw to be his proxies. I see Brian as broken, without the capacity to understand how he had plundered the children, leaving a hole that could only be filled by what he had taken from them.

Cal started to feel unmoored almost immediately in Connecticut, but although he spoke of his regret over the move, it was clear he was torn; Cal could not leave his brother. He would call me at night and whisper from the bathroom of his father's house about his feelings of desperation. Cal did not know how to fix things without unleashing his father's fury.

Weekends with Cal in New York could be turbulent—simultaneously wonderful and fraught. When he was thirteen, he refused to return to his father's house at the end of one spring weekend. He jumped out of the car when we stopped for a light; Brian was forced to drive to the city to get him. Yet despite Cal's ambivalence, the change gave us an opportunity to be different together. We had moved back into our Manhattan apartment, and Cal joined weekend soccer and basketball teams, and took singing and acting classes. He was talented, prepared diligently for auditions, and read for the venerable playwright of a Broadway play. This was the first time I had the luxury of free time in the city with Cal, and it felt like a gift.

Cal met new friends, Josh and David, at soccer and the three were together most weekends. Josh lived with his mother and David with his father. They were sensitive kids, and I think part of their connection was not having come from traditional two-parent homes. They were a force on the soccer field, all three having unfortunate hair-trigger tempers, and there was often drama on the field between them and the team they were playing against.

They went to parties downtown, three tall, handsome kids—one White, two Black—in jeans and sport shirts, and they took care of each other, always arriving home within twenty minutes of curfew. Only once in four years did their parents and I join forces when David, enamored of a girl, had slipped away from the other two. We found him in the early hours of the morning, and he was incredulous that we had been worried.

Josh and David would come to our apartment when Cal arrived on Friday night. I would cook something simple for Cal and David because they were always hungry, and Josh entertained us with his raps while they ate before going out. Josh would usually spend the night. More than once, I spent the following morning washing bed linens that bore the brunt of the boys' alcohol experimentation. In the morning, they would all meet again for soccer or a movie.

Sometimes they argued, one saying something stupid to the other, and I would mediate on the floor of our apartment or in our hallway. With regret, I saw that Cal's unhappiness about his life in Connecticut was beginning to impact his relationships and the things he had worked to build for himself. But despite their disagreements, the boys were magnificent together. Their creative and intellectual forces shone but were sporadic and had not yet taken on full intent or shape. Everything lay ahead of them.

As I think now about the light the boys gave off and what they would go on to discover, I remember the world when Jo and I were thirteen and I had longed to see something so new to my eyes that it had no history or backstory to taint its brilliance.

Cal spent the next three and a half years feeling overwhelmed and outnumbered. Our family situation made the normal angst of adolescence feel like a harpoon to his heart. His self-esteem imploded and his defenses toppled. Cal wanted to be back home with me, but his reluctance to leave his brother left him feeling helpless and without agency.

But we could do no more than be a nuisance to the court and encourage Cal to express his feelings. He tried a few times to leave and wrote letters to the court asking to return home. He said that his father had been violent to him and that he wanted to live with me and Ron. But Brian told Cal that if he returned to my home, they would lose the house he had bought shortly after the boys moved to Connecticut. Cal said it was a devil's pact. Returning to his father's house one night, he stared through the car window at the house and said, "A pile of wood for a child."

Noah's refusal to see me had stretched into the following year. He still would not speak to my parents, making the magnitude of my loss immeasurable. I felt that Brian had exacted his vengeance, that he had emptied my life of Noah and separated Noah from his mother, all with carefully crafted justifications. But Cal, in resisting Brian's attempts to alienate him from me and Ron, surprised us; he remained steadfast in the face of his father's efforts. By then Brian had fired his lawyer, represented himself in court, and hid his truest self behind tears and a persona of false victimhood.

Brian could be astute and hyper alert when the situation was the sort he could profit from. Like a cat patiently wearing down his prey, he knew that "mother" was how I defined myself. He knew this before I did, and I believe he foresaw the emotional cost that the loss of my son would exact on me. In his clarity of vision—his great strength—Brian had found a superb weapon. It is a specific pain, that of being discarded by your child. No matter which explanations were provided by therapists or the articles I read, the pain was sharp and aching at the same time. It was every kind of hurt, the dullness providing relief to the burn. And there was the shame factor. My child was alive and healthy, at an age when children need their mothers, but Noah did not want me. He was happier without me in his life, and everyone knew it. It is an unnatural state and so aberrant that other parents might shun me for fear of contagion.

In the first few months after the boys left, I would scream in my sleep. Ron would wake at the first sounds I made, and swaddling me with his long arms and legs, he would pin me into a cocoon until my terror slid away along with my physical borders. During the years of Noah's absence, the unknowability of his life was excruciating, and the sharpest pain came at night in nightmares whose content I could never access. Sleep was no longer a comfort or a sometime refuge, it was where despair ruled. Though my waking mind was kind to me, neatly ordering my thoughts and fears so I could begin again each day, at night it was a free-for-all where everything that buttressed me during the day became unmoored and I was alone in a sea of fire.

Oddly, when Noah himself appeared in my dreams, it was a salve, an antidote to the feeling of being forsaken. Noah's birthday was always a trial for me; each year on that day my defenses cracked apart. And Noah's birthday also coincided with the day he had officially left my home and moved to his father's house. Once, several years after Noah left, I dreamed of him on his birthday. In the dream, Noah's face was angelic, wide open, and he was happy. "It's okay, Mom, everything is going to be okay now," he said, "It's all over." Then he smiled at me, his beautiful brown eyes shining with love. I tried to keep myself from waking up so I could be with him longer. When I finally woke, my face was wet and I felt that I was drowning in my tears because once again, Noah had left.

The years went by, and Noah went off to college, but in my dreams of him, he was always fourteen.

Though he had disappeared from my view, he was living, sleeping, waking, dressing, becoming educated, going to the dentist, playing baseball, looking at girls, all while living without me. My need to mother felt all-encompassing, not lessening at all as the boys grew older. It was a given, like the Earth, without equivocation. This is what I did, who I was, and nothing else could rival the psychic hold of motherhood.

Some years later, I had at last achieved what I'd thought was impossible; I let Noah go. I had taught myself how to continue to mother him from a distance. I stayed in regular contact even when he would not respond. I wrote to him, I called, I asked to see him. There were two short periods when we saw each other, mostly at the urging of our reunification therapist.

Once, Noah and I had lunch together before our therapy session. He seemed strong and happy, and I was glad. He told me funny stories about his friends in his new school, and we laughed as we had so many times before. It was pure joy to sit across from him at the table.

But after two more therapy sessions, Noah said he felt we no longer needed to see the therapist, that everything that had happened had been put away in the past, and we could move forward on our own.

The therapist was skeptical. I remember him searching Noah's face, probing, asking him to explain what he felt. But Noah was firm and I, so grateful to hear his words, was foolish and agreed. Before we left, the therapist asked that we come back if we had any concerns about our relationship.

But very soon afterward Noah became distant again, making excuses for being unable to meet, until finally he told me he did not want to see me anymore. He refused to return to therapy with me. I ruminated about the lunch we had shared before the therapy session. What had I said that had derailed us again? Nothing concrete had happened to pull us backward, but I believed I knew the reason.

Brian had been upset about sharing the cost of the therapy and had resisted it forcefully for months. Noah and I returning to each other was neither a priority nor a desirable outcome for Brian. The court and my lawyer had pushed hard for it, until ten reunification sessions were scheduled. I surmised that Brian had given Noah permission to be with me and then pulled the plug when he could.

Cal came back home four years after he left. He said then that we had saved him. It was the fall of 2009 shortly after Noah had left his father's house for college, and Cal began to speak of his discontent in firmer tones. He was sixteen and tall, nearing six feet, and somehow his growth had made him less fearful of Brian. One Sunday, he refused to go back to his father's house. I contacted my lawyer, who sent Brian an email saying that Cal would not return to Connecticut.

Ten days later, we were back in court. Brian contested the change in physical custody. The attorney for the children, who

for the last few years had seemed to exhibit an increasing dis-
taste toward Brian, emerged from a room where they had been
speaking. Her eyes rolled and her voice was filled with tem-
pered disgust as she said, "Brian just offered to sell Cal to you."
She went on to explain that Brian would agree to the change in
custody if I paid his outstanding legal fees. I refused.

Within the hour, four years after Cal left, custody was
awarded back to me.

In New York, we enrolled Cal in a nontraditional private
school, many of whose students had also suffered traumas. Cal
found girls and let them hurt him; he was tender and idealistic inside and could fall in love quickly. He wrote letters to
the court about his father. He was angry that he had not been
heard, and he was still torn by conflict. He saw a psychologist
who Cal said "got" him. For years, Cal had managed to sidestep Brian's efforts to alienate him from me, but now it seemed
that everything he had held back was pouring out.

PART III

CHAPTER 28

CAL
(2011-2012)

Three years passed, and Cal had just turned nineteen. He had my generous mouth, thick hair the color of honeyed oak, and eyes the blue green of the Mediterranean under a noon sun. But he had grown depressed and frightened because he could not envision a future. His mind had turned against him, and I was heartsick. Years of battling for custody had exacted a price that Cal could not stop paying. The rest of us had moved forward in its aftermath, leap-frogging over ourselves like newly released prisoners of war. Cal said that he could have survived the first divorce, but the second, the divorce of his mother from his brother, was too much to bear.

He had graduated from high school the year before, and, after intense lobbying from me, he agreed to spend a gap year studying in Israel. Cal had been so caught up in his sadness and distress at the end of high school that he could hardly focus on schoolwork. When Cal enjoyed a subject—philosophy, history, writing—he easily shone, but his teachers were worried; everyone could see his pain. We planned trips in the sun, once to see his favorite football team play in the Midwest.

But afterward the trips seemed like exercises that had done more harm than good. The anatomy of these trips was in such contrast to Cal's inner world that they only served to pile more pain onto what he already carried.

Although Cal had been accepted to a private college, I was adamant that he must first understand what was gnawing away at him. I was afraid that the challenges of living independently at college might paralyze him. Cal disagreed, believing that if he was away from home, in a new environment, he would break free from his demons. We struck a bargain eventually, but Cal was very angry and felt betrayed by me. I finally agreed to fund a private college education if he would first attend and succeed at university in Israel for one year.

With enormous reluctance, Cal left for Israel, but it was not the panacea I had imagined for him. The noise in his head still hammered at him despite the newness and stimulation of Israel. We were saddened but not surprised when Cal refused to attend the Israeli university in the autumn. At the last moment, I extended his summer program into a full gap year, but his suffering did not subside, and he returned home.

When he returned to the United States, I asked that he stay in Connecticut with his father. I was frightened for his safety in New York. Cal had been miserable that summer in Israel, the blare growing louder until he could no longer see a life free of pain. And I could no longer see Cal's struggles as just a sporadic coincidence. I did not know the exact mechanism, but I knew that I had transmitted my pain to him.

Brian and his girlfriend wrote me letters asking that I bring Cal back to New York, saying that he needed to be with me, his mother, while he grappled with his demons. Years earlier, they had said in court that Cal should not visit us in New York because I was toxic. But Cal had frightened me in New York during his last year of school. He stayed out late, sometimes until early morning, and did not answer his phone. I knew teenagers did this, yet I lay in bed in a controlled panic, my face shoved into a pillow, a stabilizing force to counter my fear that Cal had been stabbed or pushed onto the subway tracks.

Ron and I had long occupied a disturbing place where Cal's pain loomed over us heavily, but since Cal could not say what would heal him, we alone had to construct a solution. And we had to nail it quickly; time was running out. At nineteen, Cal was officially independent but he still trusted us. Ron was never able to watch a problem worsen, and he was driven to find a solution. He barreled through Internet searches until he found what he was looking for: Matara, an educational youth program in Israel. Set in the Judean Hills on the west bank of the Jordan River, it was for boys who were not reaching their academic potential at home, kids who were caught between the expectations of others and their true selves.

The program was the brainchild of a psychologist with a healthy opinion of himself. Sometimes we thought that Dr. Lester might have become overly inflated by the idealization of the parents had he not been a pious man who felt his ultimate purpose was to serve. At times the program seemed only a few degrees away from a cult, but nowhere had we found an option for Cal that gave us more hope. It was only after the plan was conceived to send Cal to Matara that his endowment to us, the excruciating vise of worry, finally started to loosen.

Most of the boys in the program had been city-raised, and a tenet of Matara was the healing power of nature. Counselors led the boys on hikes into the northern hills of Galilee, to the Negev desert in the south, and to Eilat for scuba diving. The boys studied and worked to regain themselves by engaging with each other in the natural world. The repeated mantra was that they need not fit into grids established by people or institutions; instead, their uniqueness should be celebrated.

Freedom from lifelong demands for conformity was sweet, and the boys were taught to love and respect their singularity. The very thing they had been taught to suppress until it disappeared—their unconventional manner of learning and being in the world—was what would make them whole. Like Dorothy's quest to return home to Kansas, it was an epiphany that had been in front of them all the time. Most of the boys thrived, and revived by their new sense of self-esteem, they left to make their way in a world they saw to be more forgiving.

People asked us, "Why Israel, why so far away?" After Cal agreed to our plan, we were so grateful and relieved that we paid little attention to the reactions of others. But how did we know that Israel would be Cal's salvation, and did we know unconsciously that it could be ours as well? Was it an instinct, part of our genetic material, to know that Israel could save Cal?

The pull of Israel was visceral and insistent, the sort of sensation that arises upon hearing your infant whimper. And we were too involved with getting Cal to Israel to formulate an acceptable explanation to others. To say that we simply *felt* Israel would heal him without offering up proper evidence was reckless. With Cal's future in the balance, was this yet another example of our impulsiveness? But we believed, and still do, that Cal would have been swallowed up whole had he not gone to Israel at that point in his life.

The day arrived for Cal to fly to Israel with us. Ron and I drove from New York to Brian's house in Connecticut, and we called Cal's phone from the curb. There was no answer. After ten minutes of waiting in the car, Ron's face fell. He looked so weary—tired from all the years leading up to where we were now. Disappointment and defeat leached into his voice as he said, "That's it. He's not there—he's not coming."

I left the car and walked up the brick drive, which led to a door at the back of the house. I had already decided not to march up to the front entrance. The back door made a softer statement, and perhaps no one would notice that I was stealing my son. I rang the bell, heard it peal inside the house, and waited, breathing hard. After a few minutes with no sign of life from inside, I moved down the path and stood in front of yet another door, this one on the front porch.

This time a young girl opened the door, and I asked for Cal. She called out for him, and hearing the lilt of her childish voice, I felt enormous relief and my spirit returned. He was there! I had been afraid that Brian, in an abrupt turnaround, might have enticed Cal away from the house, perhaps with an emergency game of golf. Then I saw Cal shuffle by as if sleepwalking, holding a duffel bag into which he was pushing clothes. He looked drained of everything.

I called out from the doorway, "Cal, c'mon, let's go! We've been waiting!"

Without turning his head, he looked at me sideways, nodded, and kept moving. I went back to the car. Ron's head had been resting on the steering wheel between his hands, and he began to start the engine as I got in.

"No, Ron, Cal is in the house. He's there, he's still packing!"

"You're serious?" he asked, staring at me, his face blanching. I wanted so much to hold his head with my hands and smooth the bleakness from his face. It was as if he had been holding his breath since I left the car, not allowing any oxygenated blood to reach his skin. "I had visions of driving back to the city, miserable, having to cancel the tickets, the hotels—everything a mess. I can't believe he's there. What did he say?"

"Nothing really—with words anyway. He just looks awful, gray, walking around, half-alive. So pale."

"Not a minute too soon," Ron said staring through the windshield, fists still gripping the wheel. "Witch burners." He looked around at the pristine lawns of the street with disgust; he was exhausted already, and the day would be a long one.

Another quarter of an hour passed, and our anxiety returned. Keeping my eyes fixed on the doors that were partially hidden by bushes, I saw movement, and with another surge of relief I watched a door open. Cal walked out of the house dragging his duffel bag behind him.

I heard Ron breathing deeply next to me.

"Just get in the car, Cal," I hissed to myself. We were calm, both of us good actors, as Cal made his way into the backseat with his bag. The slam of the car door signified deliverance.

The flight to Israel was long, nearly twelve hours. Ron read, and Cal and I watched silly buddy movies, and that night, in our hotel in Jerusalem, we all slept heavily. We had made it, and everything would start the next morning when Cal would be introduced to a Matara counselor. They were to take a short hike in the Judean Hills, and afterward Cal would be driven to the home of the family he would live with. Each boy in the program stayed with a family in the small city of Ma'ale Adumim, a thirty-year-old settlement east of Jerusalem in the West Bank. The town teemed with a large, mostly orthodox Jewish population, and the stone houses were built on several levels with generous outdoor space for the town's large families.

Cal moved in with Moshe and Zelda and their grown children. He would begin to study Hebrew and, we hoped, settle into the warmth of the community's life with its Shabbat observance and close bonds between families. We started to relax. Sheltered by Moshe and Zelda, Cal was about to be ensconced in the safe harbor of Israel.

Ron and I wandered through the streets of Jerusalem. Our small hotel was on a pedestrian street that had been the site of a bomb explosion during Israel's War of Independence in 1948. On our first morning in Israel, we awoke to the clatter of shopping cart wheels on the street below our balcony. We ate breakfast at a café next to the hotel. Everything, even the food, seemed exotic; neither of us had been to Israel in decades.

Two young women in their twenties were sitting at the table next to ours. They wore patterned head scarves wrapped around hair that was pulled back and high at the crown with just an inch or two showing at the hairline. They were drinking coffee after shopping, and plastic bags loaded with fruit were splayed around the legs of the table. As my head dipped toward the ground taking in the measure of their purchases, I saw the large wheels.

One woman sat in a wheelchair. She had seen my interest, and I was embarrassed to have been caught staring, but she smiled and said, "You have such beautiful green eyes."

Her manner was shy, yet she looked directly at me. On the surface, her posture and situation were vulnerable, but the initial sympathy I felt for her disappeared when we spoke. Under her scarf, her face was luminous, and in it was a comfort of being in her skin that was incapable of inspiring pity.

Looking back at her, there was a fluttering in my chest and I felt that I had been invited to enter the marrow of this stranger and this place. We spoke for a while—I cannot remember about what—until Ron and I said our goodbyes and left. I had never felt a spiritual void or need for anything other than conscience and moral beliefs to guide me, but I believe this woman became my lodestar. What she left me with remains, and to my mind, she embodied the essence of the country.

Ron and I walked down busy Jaffa Street toward the ancient city of Jerusalem. In the hours that followed, we walked up into the hills leading to Hebrew University and Hadassah Hospital on Mt. Scopus. During Israel's War of Independence, my father's uncle Karol, an army medic, had been killed in the Hadassah medical convoy massacre. A transport of doctors, nurses, students, and patients, desperate to relieve the blockade of the hospital, was ambushed by Arab forces. Seventy-nine people were murdered.

But that time seemed long gone, and everything we saw now—university students, olive and pine trees framing and obscuring the bleached Jerusalem stone—was new, and there was something soothing but also unsettling in the murmurings of the breezes that countered the intense heat. And like the extraordinarily clear understanding one has in a dream before the inevitable forgetting, a truth was exposed. Israel was where we belonged because we were *of* this land.

I said to Ron, "I'm not sure what it is, but I feel that we are in between something here. It's so sudden, this feeling—almost out of nowhere—but I'm not sure New York is our home anymore."

He was quiet, looking past the soldier-guarded entrance of Hebrew University where the students swarmed.

"I know," he said quietly. "It doesn't make sense, but it feels like I've come home. For the first time in my life."

Something began to expand inside of me. Had Ron taken my comment on its face, we might have talked about how Israelis were different, more engaged than Americans, or how dry and scorching Jerusalem was. We could have walked on to the massive outdoor food market, or to the Israel Museum, or maybe we could have continued talking about Cal and whether this new plan for him would work, could free him.

"I don't want to leave," I said.

Ron squinted down the hill we had climbed up to Mt. Scopus. He knew where I was going before I did. We were hot and sticky, and my shirt clung under my arms. I was not used to being out so long in a white-hot sun that made us as blind as newborns. Ron looked back at me and took my fingers in his hand. He knew the way my mind worked, the circles it made. Then he nodded.

I stopped breathing and my chest rose, the air catching in my throat. I could not believe what we were contemplating, and I was afraid that in Ron's consuming need to please me, I was leading him to a place he did not want to go.

"Really, are you sure?" I asked.

"I am. Nuts, isn't it?"

And that is how it came to be, on our first day back in Israel, that we made the decision to immigrate and become Israeli citizens. Our future was decided.

CHAPTER 29

ISRAEL
(2012)

At first, Israel whispered to us. Then the whisper became a racket impossible to ignore, catapulting us so that there was nowhere else to land. Something that had been dormant in both Ron and me had come alive. Like an ether, the understanding that we had come home slipped in and around us until we became part of it. Making the decision to immigrate to Israel took far less time than we would have spent planning a vacation. I wonder sometimes—because it feels so elemental, so basic—if we were driven by a collective unconscious of inherited trauma to make our way back to the place where it had all started.

Genes do their work by expressing proteins, which in turn affect how our cells function, a dance between their inner workings and the environment. Perhaps sorrow and loss are so endemic to the Jewish experience that over thousands of years our genes "learned" to express the precise molecules that built resilience in the face of hostile environments… that we had, in complex biological and social processes, evolved to adapt to grief, to accept pain as one element of living as Jews.

In *Fiddler on the Roof*, the stage adaptation of Sholem Aleichem's tales, the Jews of Anatevka must leave their homes because violence against them is increasing. One man, exhausted by the prospect of leaving, asks the rabbi if this might be a good time for the Messiah to come. The rabbi's response is farsighted and highly adaptive: "We will just have to wait for him somewhere else. Meanwhile, let's start packing."

With these simple words the rabbi explains that, despite suffering, Jews cannot wait for deliverance, they must deliver themselves. And with his instructions to start packing, the imperative to survive and begin anew shines through.

When I saw Israel again after the passage of forty years, a new generation was in charge, and it showed. Everything seemed brighter, more colorful, more self-aware and proud. There was a devil-may-care attitude in the streets. We could not understand how Israelis, so lauded for their entrepreneurship and multitudes of startup tech companies, seemed to be doing nothing but sitting in cafés with laptops, working out at public beachside gyms, or playing volleyball on the beach. Were these venues the laboratories of Israel's innovation?

Throngs of locals, tourists, and surfers packed the Mediterranean shore, turning it into a glorious show of humanity. Its miles-long promenade was lined with palm trees and accommodated a constant flow of cyclists, joggers, and walkers. And it was where I bicycled every morning, breathing in the atmosphere of my home.

Tel-Aviv had been transformed from desert a century earlier by Zionist pioneers and then further developed by orphaned survivors of the Holocaust. Their faces, triumphant and wounded, looked out from the juxtaposed photos of past and present displayed throughout the city and on the ancient sea walls of the Jaffa Port. The tenor of the city was a combination of unrelenting forward movement and joy in the moment within the context of love for the land and homage to its history.

Steeped in the Israeli mindset was the idea that life must be embraced without reservation *now*, a natural result of living with the existential threats of terrorism and wars that came once or twice a decade. No one had forgotten Yom Kippur of 1973 when soldiers ran through synagogues thrusting sheets of paper into the hands of the rabbis, effectively ending prayers on the holiest day of the year. Fear pulsated from row to row as the rabbis called out names and synagogues throughout the country emptied as young men removed their prayer shawls and raced to join their combat units.

We were mesmerized by the soldiers. Still soft-cheeked kids, they moved through the streets in twos and threes or in packs, a sea of green or beige. Sometimes we would see a group of them wearing jeans or sundresses dawdling on their way to the beach or the mall. Moving closer, we noticed the machine guns slung across their torsos. They seemed so young, like saplings; we should have been protecting *them*. We, the middle-aged, should have been the ones checking the terror tunnels from Gaza or clearing minefields.

And as if we needed another reason to immigrate, it became clear to us that if these teenagers were willing to sacrifice themselves, then we must become part of the home front. The oath the soldiers made at their army induction included a vow to give everything, including their lives, to Israel. This security of the nation born from bottomless grief was as important as the lives of its precious children, because neither could survive without the other. There is a oneness about Israel and its people, each locked in concert with the other.

Ron had told me about an older couple he had known when he lived in the hills above Haifa with his first wife in the late 1970s. The couple had lost their only child, a son, in the

Six-Day War. Ron described the pair moving as if in a trance, the world only a proxy for the real thing, which had ended for them with the death of their child.

I thought of those parents in the morning sometimes when I saw our own neighbors leave with their little boy and snapping dog. The child had a bronchial ailment and wheezed when their cat Coco came too close. The cat was banished from their apartment and became the building's pet. Coco seemed to enjoy the life of a nomad, as he was very independent and a bully. Refusing to budge from his settled position on someone's doormat, Coco would stare and hiss when our dog leaned in for a kiss. At night, the yelps and screams of interlopers came through our open windows as Coco chased them out of the garden.

The young family would come down their concrete walk like a little pack with their knapsacks and bags, the child on his tricycle and the dog in tow. The parents were tall and athletic, with jeans that hung from nonexistent rears. It seemed as if every bit of human sustenance, whether food or air, was diverted to their child. I wondered if this mother would allow her son to join a fighting unit when the time came for him to enlist.

Before I could stop it, the image of this family in a horrific future grew. This little boy, another Israeli child taken, and the parents gone into the grave with him. All to preserve the safety of the children, the middle-aged, and the old with numbers tattooed on their arms. The mother so determined that her child would live an allergy-free life and the father remembering his own time in a war that was long over. I saw their lives empty without the one who gave them purpose, and I knew how little I understood about life in this country.

Despite the excruciating imaginary scenarios that had played in my head since childhood, I knew very little about life because I had sidestepped the greatest grief.

CHAPTER 30

A HOME ON A HILL
(2012-2013)

The apartment that would become our home was situated on a street named for Israel's first poet laureate, Chaim Bialik. In 1922 he built his house on a small hill in Tel-Aviv that at the time was mostly sand. Today, the vegetation is lush and the air steams in the summer. The older trees are gnarled, with thick trunks that push out their own miniatures from clefts of limbs near the ground. Their uppermost branches reach across the narrow streets to entangle with branches on the other side. The younger trees are slender and modest but also stretch to touch the bigger ones.

Stucco apartment buildings on our street rose from these small forests. Built in the 1920s and '30s, many were only three stories high. It was a delight to see such an abundance of sky after being desensitized to the thievery of light by Manhattan's skyscrapers. There was so much sky to see in Tel Aviv, and I loved how the stark white of the flat Bauhaus roofs met the blue sky and cut it horizontally. Each room in our apartment led to a balcony. Vines crept in through the windows, giving us a sense of living in a treehouse.

Settling in felt seamless. We were home at last, in a way that neither of us had known. People on our street wanted to know why we had come here. They would ask questions that we had always thought were too personal to be asked. When I registered for Ulpan, Hebrew language classes, the receptionist looked at me over her glasses and asked, "So, how much did you pay for your apartment?"

I learned later Israelis considered it perfectly reasonable to ask questions about home prices and salaries, even in conversations with strangers.

My mother's Orthodox fourth cousin, Benny, saw us as close family and insisted on bringing us to his home for holidays and to meet his newest baby. But Cal and Ron and I were family to each other, which gave us a base from which to reach out. What we found confirmed our earliest impressions of Israelis. They might be gruff, especially the seasoned government employees, but after a few minutes of struggling to communicate, and perhaps a minor disagreement or two, these same people opened their arms and pulled us in.

Strangers were all family, but as this was not merely an impression but a genetic truth, we felt this kinship with great immediacy and it warmed us. Sometimes when an interaction was unpleasant at first, emotions would peak and then lose steam until we said our goodbyes with an invitation to dinner. When people asked why we had immigrated, the question often felt like a test. We would respond that Israel was the answer to every question we had never known we had.

On the Jewish holidays, we received invitations to family dinners and celebrations. It seemed that even our acquaintances needed to know that we were taken care of.

Because ours was an older building, it had no bomb shelter. A few times a year when rockets were launched toward

Tel-Aviv from Gaza and sirens blared at night, we would gather in the stairway, the most structurally secure spot in the building.

Later, our downstairs neighbors made keys to their basement for all of the residents. Never had we felt so connected to people outside our family. These relationships lay somewhere between those of friends and blood relatives. It was the most wonderful space to occupy, and we never felt alone, as if the normal divisions that separated people did not apply.

Years after our arrival, during the COVID-19 pandemic, our neighbors and friends shopped for us when we were in quarantine, leaving groceries or dinner in front of our door. We would hear a quick knock, and after opening the door we saw no one but felt the shift of air particles as someone flew down the stairs.

Soon we began to live like others in tandem with the country's ethos of survival. We went to cafés, to movies, and to the beach, and we took cover when the sirens warned that a rocket launched from Gaza was heading toward us.

CHAPTER 31

MY FATHER, EDWARD
(2013)

Inconceivably, though only to me, my mother became a widow shortly after I moved to Tel Aviv. My father had been ill for a year with a blood disease that he did not research on Google and thus did not know that it was incurable. Instead, he preferred to continue traveling, and three weeks before he died, my parents embarked on a cross-country train trip. Jo met my parents in San Francisco, where she lived. In Jo's photos, she and my mother, still youthful at eighty, shone with warmth and health. But my father's face in one photo breaks me apart. He appears small as he leans with both hands on his elegantly carved cane, his pale green eyes squinting in the sun's glare. My father had always been tall, but the bones in his spine had weakened and grown soft from his illness, stealing inches of height from him. His expression says that he is leaving.

The day after my parents returned from their trip, my father caught the flu. I had come to their apartment to show him the pictures of our new home in Tel Aviv. He was so pleased that I had stopped by. Wanting me to sit next to him, he patted the mattress next to where he sat propped up with a pillow, his legs stretched out in front of him.

I scooted up next to him, and together we went through the pictures on my phone. That night, my father ran a high fever. The next day he was admitted to the hospital and then to the Intensive Care Unit. When, from my seat in the waiting area, I saw a doctor race down the corridor, I knew where he was going. My father had suffered a massive heart attack, and the doctor told us that he could not breathe on his own anymore.

Grief made my mother seem lost, like a little girl. My dad was not conscious, and my mother lay her head on his chest as the ventilator breathed for him. In their cocoon on the bed, my mother tried, through the weight and force of her body, to keep my father from leaving. And I remembered a resplendent pair blazing with life. Photos showed them on ski slopes, grabbing tree branches on Appalachian mountain trails, in blue waters, in Europe on bikes, grinning, happy, arms slung over each other's shoulders. Alive.

Another photo, taken at their wedding. The photographer caught my parents in profile, the camera fixing them in dark silhouette against a white backdrop. My mother reaches to kiss my father's mouth and her neck swans upward. My father's head is bent to receive her kiss, and their hands are intertwined.

Sixty years later, in a hospital room, my mother whispered into my father's ear and stroked his parched skin. Kissing his face, navigating tubes and wires, she climbed further onto the bed. The doctor said that once the ventilator was disconnected, my dad would be gone quickly. I picked up his hand and pressed his palm to my cheek, willing myself to remember the feel of my father's hand on my face.

At three o'clock in the morning, the room was dark except for the indicator lights of the machines. The hospital room had a terrible eeriness about it, and we were all sinking, the gloom mirroring the collective despair in the room. I cannot think that it would have been easier to let him go in the daylight.

I called Noah, who was then living and working in North Carolina, and I put my phone on speaker mode and held it to my father's ear. Noah told his grandfather, his adored Papa since the very beginning, that he loved him. And when my father was gone, I unstrapped the watch he had worn to the hospital, kissed it, and put it on my wrist.

At home, on his desk, were two plane tickets to Croatia for their next trip. We brought my mother to Israel afterward, but she was at an unknown juncture and needed to go back home to see who she would be without her Eddie.

CHAPTER 32

A BEAUTIFUL ANIMAL
(2015-2017)

In the beginning, our children had not understood our decision to immigrate to Israel. They felt we were being impulsive, which was true. What they did not know was that impulse can become wise over time.

When Ron and I married after six months together, it seemed like undue haste to some, but what we felt for each other concurred with what our rational minds believed about marriage, children, and the people we wanted to be. Our emotions, thoughts, and values were closely aligned, so our decision to marry was informed by what we intuitively longed for in a mate, and what, after our past failures, we knew to be crucial for a marriage to succeed.

The apparent rashness of our Aliyah was in fact our realization that Israel was the aggregate of over half a century of mourning for those who had perished in the Holocaust, and a yearning for our souls to be made whole. It was the opposite of impulse. Ron and I recognized Israel as we had recognized each other.

Soon after our move, the children came to visit; they wanted to make sense of the new life we had chosen. Noah came to see his brother for a long-awaited reunion. Our sweet golden retriever, Chloe, had taken ill with a terrible suddenness and had died before we could bring her to Israel, but Dolce was still strong and able to tolerate the long flight.

We were three in Israel, and then we met a big white dog. I first saw him at the animal hospital where we had taken Dolce to see her neurologist. We were learning that dogs in Israel had specialists—neurologists, cardiologists, and internists—and this made us feel very secure. The white dog lay in a heap on the floor in front of the receptionist's desk. His chin rested on his front paws, which were crossed elegantly in front of him. He looked up occasionally to make sure that Vered, the receptionist, was still there.

The dog lifted his head up and to the side, slowly looking around with obvious discomfort, and after seeing that nothing had changed, settled back into his sad pose. I rose from the worn cushions of the waiting room bench and lay down on the floor next to the dog on the edge of the gray cloth that had been placed underneath his stomach. His fur was the white of week-old snow and he was shaved from belly to tail. How awful he looks, I thought. He is ugly, but he is in pain.

"Whose dog is this?" I asked Vered.

And she told me his story. He had been taken from his owner's garden where he had been kept in a cage that he had outgrown, which had forced the big dog to arrange his bones more and more awkwardly until his head and long nose had no place to go but to rest on his chest. The dog had been born without properly functioning hip joints, and his dysplasia was so extreme that his legs were nearly useless and walking could send him into spasms.

The man who took the dog was David, a roguish fellow who ran a covert nonprofit organization that rescued abused animals. He lived nearby and grew angry seeing the beautiful dog crammed into a cage that looked as if it were getting smaller every time he passed the owner's garden. David enlisted the help of his old army friend, Shmuel, and together they hatched a plan.

From his paratrooper days, David remembered that the night was darkest before dawn broke, so he and Shmuel planned to arrive then. They parked the car behind the owner's house near the fenced backyard. Lights off, engine on, dog-napping tools in their hands, the men quietly left the car. The place had already been cased, so they knew their entry and exit points, which were the same. The men wore black and moved stealthily. Shmuel clutched a piece of hamburger behind his back. David was driving the getaway car and could not risk getting bitten.

The dog was sleeping, curved into a letter C, his big black nose pressed into a soft spot over his feeble hip joints like a duck with his beak nestled into his feathers. Hearing the soft crunch of the men's feet on the wet grass, the animal's ears alerted and he watched their approach. Hunger was an ongoing state, and he was used to people handling food around him, so he did not presume that the meat he smelled was for him. But as the man's hand came closer, he wondered. Then, fingers pushed through the small squares of the cage's grating.

The men opened the latch, and there was nothing now between the dog and freedom. He didn't move or reach for the meat. His fur was matted with feces, and David and Shmuel winced at the smell as together they crouched toward the dog with the blanket they had brought. David readied the cloth to tuck around him while Shmuel offered him the meat. The dog was so tightly jammed in the cage that they had to move slowly to avoid twisting his limbs. Once he was extracted, they ran, pushed the dog into the backseat of the car, and drove off.

They brought him to Noga, who volunteered at an animal rescue shelter. She took the dog to a surgeon friend at the animal hospital who scheduled a complicated procedure to rebuild the dog's hip joints. After the surgery, Noga took him home to recuperate. But the dog couldn't walk, and he lay on her bed and cried all day from the pain. After two weeks of carrying the seventy-pound animal to the garden to relieve himself, and on the edge of physical collapse from the demands of her own animals and her day job, Noga again reached out to one of her contacts. The dog was delivered to the animal hospital, where he received hydrotherapy during the day and slept at night in the recovery room. It was at this point in the dog's life that we met.

"It's so sad," Vered said, looking over her reading glasses at the dog lying on his belly. His front legs, now uncrossed, spread out like wings, his elbows jutting from his body at right angles. "He has no one, and he's depressed. I wish I could take him home, but Lola, my dog, is such a bitch, I couldn't leave them alone together."

Ron had been watching me from the bench with a suspicious look on his face as he waited for the vet to examine Dolce.

"Ron, what do you think about bringing him home for Shabbat?"

He looked down at the sad dog and said, "Hmm, just for Shabbat? Right."

We brought him home and named him Wilbur, and now we were four in Israel. Dolce did not bother much with Wilbur; she probably thought him odd because he was too frightened to move from our foyer for weeks. There, we fed him his meals and gave him his medications until he felt safe enough to venture out of the hallway.

Wilbur's fur grew in where he had been shaved, and as he relaxed into his new life, I noticed that he was not ugly at all, but quite beautiful. I dragged him into the shower with me and kept his fur the color of freshly fallen snow. He allowed me to brush his teeth, eyeing me warily but never biting, while I pried open his alligator mouth. After he ventured from the foyer to explore parts unknown in the rest of the apartment, Wilbur examined the kitchen, the living room, and finally our bedroom, where he jumped onto the bed, pushed and pulled the quilt into a soft pile, stretched out diagonally, and went to sleep, snoring loudly.

I was happy whenever I looked at him because, unlike the broken pigeon I had found in Central Park a lifetime before, the wings of this beautiful creature had been saved.

Every six months or so, Ron's daughter Lea would visit, but mostly she came to spend time with Dolce. Part of her brain had always been reserved for Dolce. With Dolce, Lea could breathe, and she was her truest self with her dog. Enveloping Dolce in her arms, Lea whispered tender words into her ears. They would sit together on the floor until Dolce began to fidget or Lea would get a stitch in her back.

But Ron's love for Dolce was something otherworldly. She was his dearest, his *raison d'être,* I thought sometimes. Ron believed Dolce to be of the noblest and most mythic character. Her physical being to him was wondrous, exquisite beyond comparison and description. To Ron, she was the epitome of pure Dog, a title granted to only the most statuesque and dignified members of the species. He had written her a love letter that he kept in his top desk drawer in an envelope on which he had scrawled:

DOLCE. OPEN IN AN EMERGENCY ONLY

"When all is done here, please come seek me out, use all your keen intuition and that sense of smell. Be the clever, intelligent, and stubborn dog that you are and come find me out there in the cosmos. I will be waiting."

Lea and Ron took Dolce to the beach to swim almost every day, and from time to time I would join them. Wilbur and I did not like the sand. One afternoon, I watched them in the water from the shore. Ron held Dolce in his arms as they rested from their play while Lea treaded water in circles around them. Ron and Dolce were chest-deep, and locked together they gave the impression of being one as the sea moved them along. Dolce's chin skimmed the water, and her paddling feet were visible underneath in the clear water as Ron held her belly. Ron's face was full of sadness. Dolce was almost fifteen and Ron could not stop thinking about the day when she would leave us. He felt his heart could never again be opened this wide or hold such a vastness of feeling.

It was in moments like this, when we were simply living, that astonishment edged away whatever I was thinking. Astonishment at this life-changing thing we had done, and with it a sense of fullness, as if nothing was lacking, as if there was nothing left to aspire to. It was all here on this sand, and though I still lived with Noah's absence, I knew my child was healthy and alive, and that was my comfort.

Pulling my hat lower on my head and saluting the sky to shield my eyes from the low-hanging sun, I kept track of my family. They seemed to be further out now, but I was not worried because the water did not deepen for a few hundred meters and the sea was very calm. Breakers landing low on an angle to the shore were turned into silver mirrors by the sun—one after the other like a ravishing chorus that repeats and repeats. Six months later, Ron held Dolce as they bade each other goodbye, their eyes closed, their noses touching.

CHAPTER 33

ANOTHER ALIYAH, LONG AGO (2017-2018)

Spring in Israel is lush and dry at the same time. I am on a bus that is speeding from Jerusalem toward Tel Aviv; an impatient Israeli cowboy is driving. I stare through the window at the receding hills as the villages to the east come into focus. From this distance, the houses resemble a jumble of stone boxes.

I was thinking about my mother's meeting with the Jewish Agency in New York; she had decided to immigrate to Israel. I checked my phone for her update and tried to stand back. It was an enormous step for her. My mother had been nearly broken from our family's first attempt to immigrate to Israel. It was a vision she had cultivated since the end of the war, and in 1972 she brought us to Israel. My grandparents, Rose and Abraham, moved to Tel-Aviv shortly before we did.

But my mother was knocked to the ground when she faced the reality of our move. It was autumn and she stayed in New York a few months after my father and I left for Israel. He had a new job to begin, and I was to begin my studies at Tel Aviv University. My father thrived in Israel meeting other new

immigrants from around the world, who, like him, were pas-
sionate about music and literature. And I became immersed
in the life of an "olah," a new immigrant, or literally "one who
rises." We took road trips to far points in Israel, and relatives
kept tabs on us, inviting us to their homes for meals and Shabbat. We enjoyed our bohemian interim life as we waited for my
mother and brother to join us.

At university, I met students from far-flung nations. The
ones from the Soviet Union were loving, irreverent, passion-
ate, and freewheeling. Their extraordinary resilience and
humor was a balm for any unpleasantness, and from them I
learned to appreciate vodka, which Itzik from St. Petersburg
brought to school, along with hard-boiled eggs to cushion the
effects of the alcohol.

I met idealistic teenagers whose parents had sent them away
from the cloistered and increasingly anti-Semitic environment of
certain nations in South America. Others had immigrated from
South Africa, guided by Zionism and a hatred of apartheid. It
was also the first time I had met "Mizrachi" Jews who had been
expelled from Egypt, Yemen, Iraq, and all the predominantly
Arab nations to the east. The exodus of 800,000 Jews had followed
Israel's declaration of statehood. The Arab countries in which
they had lived for centuries became inhospitable in the extreme,
declaring war against the fledgling state of Israel. University was
the greatest melting pot of Jews I had ever known. It often seemed
that the education I received from my new friends was richer and
more nuanced than what I was learning in the classroom.

With the arrival of my mother and brother, everything
seemed to change. The home in Queens that my mother had
been so ready to leave, to be a pioneer in Israel, now called
to her incessantly. Our modest house, whose garden she had
tended, whose bricks and walls she had painted, had become
home to her only *after* our move to Israel.

Her tears, agony to us all, would not stop until my father agreed to return to America. From that point forward, every move my parents subsequently made was traumatic for my mother, and for weeks afterward she would sink into despair, desperate to regain the keys to the home she had left behind. After I found therapy in my twenties, my mother also began to see a therapist who helped her understand that the grief of losing her home at age six still inhabited her, rearing its head at times of loss and change.

My father was decisive and could not bear to see my mother brokenhearted. Following the decision to return to New York, the peace I'd had in Israel left me. My thoughts turned against me then, and it was only later that I could grasp how my ability to ward off this destructive process weakened when I was challenged by quickly changing circumstances. Somewhere in the depths of my unconscious, I believe I concluded that having repetitive ugly thoughts was more palatable than experiencing the *feeling* of anger towards my mother. But I resented her abrupt turnabout. I loved my mother deeply, and our relationship was mostly honest, but I could not tolerate having negative feelings towards her. Again, there had to be something wrong with *me* to have caused her pain.

I spent most of the year wading through self-recrimination. These thoughts grew more painful and paralleled my mother's growing depression over her own sudden pivot and the upset it had caused her parents, who refused to leave Israel.

I did not know how to question the authority of my ruminations or the degree to which I was psychologically enmeshed with my mother. I made no connection between what I felt and what she had experienced. Unaware that her turmoil was affecting me, I externalized my unhappiness to focus on things around me rather than inside me. Not comprehending the fact that I took myself with me wherever I went, I felt relieved to return to the United States.

I believe that the specter of my mother's regret after her years of purpose and effort frightened me. There was so much to plan for that my parents did not see how rootlessness had overtaken me. It may have been my mother's childhood echoing around us, but my solution was to latch on to fears that harm would come to my family, fears that in their great familiarity felt like home. In turning my sadness around leaving Israel against myself, I buried all my muddy emotions underground rather than experience them. I did not know any other way.

My mother continued to urge her parents to return to New York with us. My grandparents lived on a commercial street, strangely empty of trees, cafés, and markets, with little of the green, honeyed Tel Aviv I loved. My grandmother Rose was homesick for Sunnyside, but Abe flat-out refused to leave. He was frightened that the monthly payment of $300 he and Rose received in reparations from the German government would disappear if they returned to the United States. No amount of pleading from my mother could shake my grandfather's conviction that they would lose the income they depended upon to live.

"Why would they stop, Papa? They have no reason to cut off the checks!"

"Do not tell me what the Germans can do!" he roared. "I have seen them at their worst, and I won't risk losing what we live on!"

Following our return to the United States, my mother agonized about what she viewed as the fallout of her decisions. Besieged by feelings that she had abandoned her parents, my mother developed a visceral dislike of Tel Aviv, as if she tasted something foul whenever she visited her parents.

My grandmother appeared to be impervious to illness, but my grandfather's six decades of smoking had so cobwebbed the tissue of his lungs that oxygen could barely pass through, and he was suffocating. As a child, I would stay a safe distance away while my mother, aunt, and grandmother stood in a huddle outside the bathroom door, yelling at my grandfather who was inside, as the curling cigarette smoke escaped from the gap at the bottom of the door. My grandfather would yell back at them, demanding that the crazy women give him some privacy.

In the summer of 1977, my mother received an early morning phone call from my grandmother. Abe was in the hospital. I stood at the door of the bathroom as my mother wept in the shower, the scene lodged in my mind. The sounds she made were anguished, and her hands became fists flailing at the shower curtain as she cried out to something or someone unseen.

"No, no, no. Please not yet, not yet, don't let him go yet! Please, it's too soon!"

Ever the soldier, she flew that same day to Israel.

My grandfather waited for his younger daughter to arrive. He lay dying in a hospital where nurses with cigarettes hanging from their lips fitted his oxygen mask. After the traditional seven-day mourning period of Shiva, my mother brought Rose back to New York where, until the age of 101, she would live in the embrace of her daughters.

Now, living in Israel with Ron decades later, I wanted my mother to join us in Tel-Aviv, but I saw that her heart was not in it. While I had been living my own life, my mother had become truly *American*, more than I had thought was possible for a Holocaust survivor to become. And I grappled with this: How could she feel secure on any ground but the soil of Israel? And what kind of a daughter was I to leave my mother alone in New York? I felt she *had* to be with us in Israel.

CHAPTER 34

NOAH AND CAL BECOME MEN
(2018-2021)

My complete preoccupation with Cal, and the subsequent shrinking of my world, ultimately forced me to let go of both my children. When I say I "let go," I mean that I let them fly away from me. I could not save Cal if he did not want to be saved. Nor could I save Noah by acting on the assumption that he needed his mother in precisely the ways I believed he did.

Both of my boys had needed me in ways specific to their trauma from the divorce and its aftermath—in real time as the events occurred. But as the years passed, clearing away the radioactive dust of the custody battle, I saw that I had become irrelevant to the happiness of both my boys. The realization was initially agonizing, but soon, as if with the greatest exhale of my life, everything shifted.

In my center, there was a bruised spot where the boys had left their marks. It was the same place I knew myself as *mother*. From there the love for my children sprang and could not be shut down after they left, and I felt a constant awareness of the emptiness of that place. It was a raw, unhealed spot that could not be reached to be soothed.

With time and some guilt, I became more open to receiving the love of Ron's daughters and allowing them to fill that place. I had been with them for fifteen years, and "stepmother" was a moniker I did not like, so I started referring to myself as their second mother. Lea and Camille, with their childish, then adolescent, and finally adult imperatives, were impervious to our lack of biological connection and made me feel that I was still a mother. It took me years to accept my importance to them.

During times when Lea and I clashed, I retreated from her as I had always done after being injured by someone I loved. But Lea refused to let me withdraw. Furious, eyes blazing, she would say to me, "You don't get to choose to leave our relationship! You don't get to say we're not family!"

I would have escaped into my shell had she not barred the door. The girls were volatile and magical, unsteady yet determined, unsure but completely certain of what they needed, and had no qualms about letting me know exactly what I was doing wrong. And they gave me unending amounts of love. We would sit squashed together, two or three of us on a couch, at a family gathering. They had little interest in physical boundaries, like puppies who could not get close enough.

And they examined me carefully. Once, only a couple of years into our new family, I noticed Camille staring at the top of my head.

"What is that, Rena?" she said pointing to my hair. It was more of an accusation than a question.

I knew she was referring to my barely visible gray roots.

"I don't like that, Rena. Fix it, please." She was genuinely concerned that I might be regarded as less than elegant, or worse, careless with my personal upkeep.

Lea was more hands-on, preferring to groom me as if I was her baby orangutan. She would sit very close and stare, then she'd come closer to my face and either comment happily on the state of my skin, or her fingers would reach out and land on a blemish or wrinkle, demanding to know its exact provenance and the time and date of its appearance.

When we first moved to Israel, I over-enjoyed the Middle Eastern food and gained weight. When Lea noticed this on her first visit, she insisted on an intervention. I lost the weight quickly because I could not stand the scrutiny of her eyes that missed nothing.

Lea and Camille were reluctant to talk about Noah and Cal, nor would they comment on or question the changes our marriage and custody battle had brought to their family: how their lives had become different, and how their father had become obsessed with protecting me throughout the custody process.

They never complained when we traveled or when Ron missed Lea's Friday afternoon field hockey games because he would not allow me to drive alone to Connecticut. They saw no need to dwell on problems for which there was no solution, but they witnessed my pain. Lea, an adult now, absolutely refused to engage in what she termed "drama," yet she gathered me once into her arms as I cried over Cal. I will never forget the feel of her long arms encompassing me while I dissolved, our roles reversed; she took some of the pain away.

Their care did not grow from my attempts to be the perfect stepmother, but more likely from our arguments. I had decided early in my relationship with Camille and Lea that I would not hold back to keep the peace, so there has been plenty of discord over the years. But today when we chat or text, they are so alert to how I feel that it frightens me, as if they see something that I am blind to. If my sentences do not end with an upward lilt, or if my text lacks an exclamation mark, one of them will interrupt her current self-reflections and say, "Are you okay? What's going on with you?"

It continues to be difficult for me to feel their love, even when they wrap their arms around me and refuse to let go until I hug back properly, with gusto. "Rena! NO! Not like that!" Camille will admonish. "Both arms, please!"

They love directly from their hearts, the wealth of it flying past their conscious minds. How I envy their spontaneity. I know it is desirable and healthy to focus on the good things, to believe that I deserve the love, but still I cannot relinquish the idea that I am most vulnerable when I let down my guard down, even for a moment. When I tell my therapist this, she responds, "That's Holocaust thinking."

Cal remained in Israel, but with enormous ambivalence. He missed his brother and his friends Josh and David. I had urged him to study history at Hebrew University in Jerusalem where he had been in the overseas program. Whenever Cal would write or speak about the ancient world, his phrasing and descriptions of long-buried events made me feel that I was watching history unfold. Cal's ability to animate what had been gone for centuries was astonishing, and I thought that he would be an inspirational teacher.

But he was not ready to go back to school, and though it was yet another difficult lesson for me to learn, I finally understood that Cal's life was not mine to chart.

He and I often argued when we were together. I saw Cal as endowed with strengths that he discounted, strengths that I believed could take him through life's trials. I thought he needed to explore how he would live his life, what his critical purpose would be. Feeling that he had been so wounded by the divorce and its aftermath in family court, Cal believed he had to make an emotional pilgrimage before he could go forward.

My rebuttal to this thinking was that he would recover only when he moved ahead with his life. That the very process of living, being productive and distracted, and even the act of giving would force any wounds that were still open to close. But Cal felt that I was interfering in his healing, while I thought he was avoiding making adult decisions. Both analyses had merit, but Cal was the only one who could live his life and look back on it from his own perspective. His view was narrow and personal, and no matter how often we would repeat stories about youngsters who had been dealt horrific hands and triumphed, Cal insisted that his was a situation and a hurt unlike any other.

I know that this was his truth, but I was tormented by the thought that our family's struggles might shape his life into a future defined by trauma—as mine had been. I latched onto any sign that Cal felt peace or pleasure, which would instantly relieve me of guilt and fear for his future.

"See, Cal is just fine. He has recovered and will be happy from now on."

When Cal was a child, sometimes he would wake up screaming. When he was an infant, he had cried from the pain of colic, but this was different; Cal wept as if his soul was being frayed. As if there was nothing grounding him inside his body, as if he battled an enemy against whom he had no power. Exquisitely sensitive, Cal was guided from within. Most of what he decided he needed was the result of what he felt rather than what he reasoned.

His sensitivity and reactions to people, to what happened to him, reminded me of my own experiences. It is likely that through the compounding of epigenetics and my mothering, Cal had inherited from me an outsized emotional range that could become untenable in the face of stress.

When I would find stress to be intolerable, the only thing that would lower my emotional temperature was to act. Often a problem felt insurmountable, and I was unable to think through it, to reason out a solution. I feel guilt that I might have passed this on to Cal. Yet, just as I have learned to live with and accommodate my own peculiarities, I have seen Cal experience joy and meaning despite profound anxiety, especially when he was with his brother.

Once, when he was five, Cal came with me to my office after kindergarten. In a back room with desks and computers, there was a soda machine. Cal stared at the huge machine as if it dispensed liquid gold.

"Mama, do you have money? Look! You can get soda. Right here." He chose orange soda, and when the can tumbled down, he reached his hand into the tight space and pulled it out. He held the can with both hands, gazing at it with joy.

"Shall I open it, Cal?" I asked him.

"No," he said seriously, "I'm going to wait for Noah."

"But Noah won't be home from school for a long time."

"That's okay; he'll be happy."

Later, after Noah climbed off the school bus, Cal showed him the can. We went back to the office and the boys sat at a table, facing each other. Cal handed Noah the can—the prize— and I poured a plastic cup full of the orange stuff for Cal. His eyes were on Noah as he lifted the cup slowly, carefully, toward his face. Breathing deeply, Cal synchronized the touching of the cup to his mouth with Noah's sips from the can. Cal's lips made careful, determined contact with the liquid, but he never diverted his gaze as his brother drank from the can, watching the spectacle of bubbles disappear from the top.

CHAPTER 35

COMING BACK, SLOWLY

I want to believe that during the time we were absent from each other's lives Noah did not doubt my love and was fed by it. After graduating from college, Noah moved to Manhattan for work, and sometimes we would meet. I was aware that each time could be the last, and I would pull him close. This seemed to alarm Noah, and he would become very still in my embrace. My arms tight around his shoulders, I stood on tiptoe to lay my cheek on his. I needed to smell him before he retreated, breaking the embrace, and I drank him in with all my senses.

These meetings were not comfortable for either of us. Noah seemed so hesitant, so restrained with me. I could not tell if it was to protect himself or if he had grown more reserved in the years since he had left. I longed for that unselfconscious comfort of *being* with my child, which I had taken for granted. Noah had come from my body, and though it had always been a biological given, the ease we'd had in the past had left us.

When I would visit New York, Noah and I would occasionally meet after work at a small restaurant. We would each have a glass of wine; Italian red wine from Piedmonte was his favorite. How did he acquire such a specific taste? It was odd to think that I had sailed right past Noah's teenaged interest in alcohol, only to be discussing the provenances of wine with him now, when he was twenty-five. But the way we conversed was also strange, and it seemed we were at cross-purposes. Deconstruction of the entirety of what had occurred ten years before was a necessity for me, but Noah did not want this. What he wanted, *needed*, was for me to apologize and take full responsibility for the harm done to him and to Cal.

For years, I was torn. If in fact Noah could emotionally return to me following such a blanket apology, would the end justify the means? But I was one part of our family's unhappiness. I thought that to apologize for everything would be false and impede Noah's eventual understanding of what had happened in our family. But offering such an apology might give me a second chance with him: an opportunity to remake our relationship. A prospect that I frantically grasped for each time Noah gave me an opening, a bit of hope.

But I did apologize for not understanding the terrible extent of Noah's despair as we merged the families following my marriage to Ron. I told Noah that in my urgent and myopic need to ensure that we would succeed as a newly blended family, I could neither see nor ease Noah's suffering. In this context, naturally Noah would turn to his father for support and advice, but in a different scenario with a healthier father, I believe that the result would not have been the shattering of our family.

In hindsight, I see the pitted road Noah and I have taken. The constant fits and starts, the exhilaration when I would see him, and the agonizing fall when, for the sake of his emotional stability, Noah had to step back from me. I was learning piecemeal that I had to respect his cautiousness and to accept his pace, which was more tentative than mine. But how could we rebuild if so much of what had happened remained unexamined? I was finally *with* my son but could not speak to him about what had nearly destroyed me. The omissions were like a black hole gaping between us, absorbing all that we had been to each other.

He could not bear to talk about Ron, the one who had put me back together. Noah and I bore our scars differently, but we had been wounded by the same events, and both of us endured what remained of them in our minds. I think at times it all became too much of a burden for Noah, and that was when he might pull away. In his refusal to be defined by his family's past, there were periods when he needed distance from me. But we were mother and son, and I have the sense that we both took comfort in the permanence and the veracity of this biological connection that could never be taken from us.

When we would meet, I often could not keep myself from staring into Noah's eyes; he did this also, until embarrassed, we both looked away. These searching looks were our truth-telling in the absence of unwrapping all that we had done to each other, all that had been done *to* us, all the missteps we had made. Despite the hits I took, I understood it was the collateral damage of being alive, but Noah was too new in the world to know this.

Noah could not accept that his father had hurt me. Brian had told the boys that I was lying, and I believe Noah needed to see me as someone who would never accuse his father of brutality. I often think about an incident that happened in the winter of 1993, when Noah was fifteen months old. I came home that afternoon to hear Brian screaming. I was in the middle of my pregnancy with Cal.

Through the doorway to Noah's room, I saw Brian's body hunched over the changing table, his face inches from Noah's. Brian was yelling obscenities. Noah was silent, but his eyes were wide as he stared at Brian.

I moved quickly, coming between them. I said, "Let me finish."

"He pissed on me!" Brian said, shaking.

"That happens sometimes," I said. "He's a baby. He doesn't know."

How did Noah's fifteen-month-old brain interpret this explosion and the rage coming from his father? He already had some language, understood many words, but I could not imagine how Brian's behavior would be comprehended by a baby without fear and distrust as its by-products. It may well have been this incident that laid the foundation for Noah's awareness—perhaps never conscious—that safety with his father would always be conditional.

Later, I cursed my cowardice because I had not knocked Brian out. If I could go back there, would I have? I had never touched Brian in anger, yet I can see my arm rearing back, the other grabbing his shirt front and smashing his face in. A bloody, broken pit.

One question remains and never leaves me: Should I have left at that moment? How could I have thought that this was not a harbinger of future fallout from Brian's anger? Or that this was yet another one-off? On some level, I had to realize that if Brian was unchecked, my children could be harmed. Yet my defense was to believe I was the source of Brian's upset, and therefore if I improved my behavior, his anger would disappear.

But here was proof that Brian's anger was not directed solely at me, yet I refused to acknowledge it. Noah did what babies are supposed to do. There was little that could be viewed as more natural and innocent, yet it had incited Brian's rage. The reality that played out in front of my eyes ran counter to my belief that I was the *only* one who deserved to receive Brian's violence. But if he was culpable, I would have to leave. It seems that my need to hold onto such a warped view was a function of inherited Holocaust trauma still exerting its force on me: a conviction that there was something innately broken in Jews, and by extension, in me.

And there was another paradox to navigate. A springtime photo of Brian and Noah shows a laughing Brian in his softball uniform raising six-month-old Noah up high so that they are nearly nose to nose. Noah's plump legs hang and stretch, and his face is ablaze with joy. I keep this photo secured in my mind to call upon when I forget how unfathomable the human heart can be.

I was fully absorbed by shock and pain when Noah left, and I was angry at him. He was fourteen and should have had doubts about the direction his father was taking him. I thought of myself at that age—it was the time of my father's accident, when I had faced the real possibility of losing him. But I'd had two parents who would have put themselves in the line of fire for their children and would never have pitted us against each other. What I learned after integrating the loss of Noah, after the lacerating pain had subsided and a less acute derivative had settled itself inside me, was that Noah had not had a choice.

The need for a parent's love and protection is hardwired into a child, primal and all-encompassing. But the fidelity that Brian demanded in return required Noah to cut himself off permanently from me, his grandparents, and even his dog. How does the severing of lifelong bonds affect one's true self, which from birth evolved from the thousands of impressions and interactions with those who are beloved?

I know what had unraveled from my soul when Noah left, but what of the burden on his heart and mind and emotional life when I was banished? What to do with all the loving memories his brain contained of us? I took comfort in knowing that if my children believed in anything, it was the steadfastness of my love.

But Brian was built differently from me, and I think the boys were aware of his emotional fragility. I see Brian as a vulnerable child, needing so much more than had been given to him. This failing of love can snake through generations. I cannot know for certain the family dynamics during Brian's earliest years, but I can imagine that insecurity marked his childhood. For had he experienced nurturance and support during times of hurt and struggle, I think Brian would have been incapable of behavior that resulted in Noah's loss of his relationship with me. A healthy, devoted parent would have seen such an estrangement as anathema, or at the very least an undesirable consequence of parental discord.

I am not certain that Brian consciously knew what he was doing to Noah, but I do believe that rage determined his actions. Brian's pain over the divorce and my remarriage may have become more tolerable as he saw himself as Noah's only beloved parent and me as the harmful parent. The sadness I feel for Brian pales in the face of the agony and rage I feel over Noah's loss of me. Will this loss torment him later when he is a father, when I am no longer alive and cannot allay his grief?

I had resisted Noah's requests that we maintain a perfunctory relationship. I wanted so much more; I wanted motherhood in all its colors back again. But as I continued to think about how parental alienation in childhood affects the adult, I realize that reconciliation must take place on Noah's terms. He was the victim; he survived and like all survivors, he must piece his way back into a world that failed to protect him. And I will live with the knowledge that I failed Noah because I did not prevent what happened, nor did I save him, as another mother, one stronger and less fearful, might have.

Noah married and moved to the West Coast. His wife is a lovely woman who seems kind and deeply driven by her values. They love each other; I saw this on the few occasions we were together. Noah had wanted me and my mother to meet his wife, and we had dinner together a couple of times. I was usually anxious, wanting to pack so much into two hours. My mother was relaxed, and she and Noah's wife liked each other immediately and seemed happy to fill the air with getting-to-know-each-other conversation. Noah was reserved, and I would alternate between anxious chatter and silence. But our eyes searched for what might be hidden.

Over the years Noah seemed to change in great leaps. I experienced him in a way most parents do not as their children move through stages of development. As Cal grew, I could not pinpoint exactly when he began to look more like a man than a boy. Being with Cal every day, I did not see the metamorphosis in his face. But like a film sped up to show a flower transition from bud to bloom that could be stopped at pivotal intervals, I saw exactly how Noah had changed. It was like looking at photographs taken of him once each year. Noah's cheeks became less full as his face grew angular, and his eyes became more almond-shaped. His cheekbones sat high like his father's, but his mouth, like Cal's, was mine. Noah had sprouted, becoming tall and rangy, and every time I see him I want to spoon food into his mouth as I did when he was in his high chair. Each time I hug him, I remember the day he left, the day he turned fourteen, how I wept and could not let go.

Noah today is strong and loving, a man who believes in being guided by what is just and fair. Sometimes he seems to expect too much of himself, and I want to say to him: Learn what it is *you* need in this life, and give it freely to yourself. You have come through the fire, with everything that matters still intact.

CHAPTER 36

UNDERSTANDING
(2017-2021)

I found a therapist in Jerusalem who had her own ideas about what ailed me. Rhonda is a psychologist who has spent years treating victims of terrorist attacks and abuse. To me, she gave the diagnosis of obsessive-compulsive disorder, which worked in tandem with what I inherited of my parents' history.

Rhonda laid out a map of the terrain in my brain, a maze that I had spent my life running through. She taught me to stop running, to stop avoiding, to stop checking that I was safe. In her office in Jerusalem, I learned how massive a task it would be to accept that I could not control for danger or catastrophe. That if I kept running from it, danger was no farther away, and fear did not recede but spread. It took some years, but I worked hard and integrated new ways of thinking that calmed the anarchy in my head.

Though obsessing about what I could not control was a useless, brutal exercise, it may have been protective, helping to shield me from feeling too close to the pain of my parents' history as survivors. Perhaps ruminating on the possibility that a stranger would breach the front door of our home functioned to keep the flesh-and-blood reality of the Holocaust away. The fight-or-flight part of my brain that would normally be on alert for errant trucks and tigers was, I'd learned in therapy, hypervigilant.

My anxiety will never be completely assuaged, but I am learning to discern real from illusory peril and move on. Some of my earliest exposures to the aftermath of the war took place before I could properly understand the context, and I believe that this caused the watchful aspects of my mind to become overly reactive.

One of the first things I did in therapy was recognize that there was no need to give in to or heed the frightening thoughts; rather, I could view them as anomalies passing through my mind. Only my acceptance that what I feared most was possible could break the cycle. If I did not accept this reality and continued to struggle for absolute control, my anxiety would become a hungry beast requiring more and more reassurance to be satisfied, and then only temporarily.

I struggled to accept this truth, but once I did, life became sharper and sweeter, and in my mind's eye, I saw chains coming loose. I learned to starve the beast. And with that, I came to live in the world with less vigilance.

ISRAEL INDEPENDENCE DAY, 2021

In 2021 we celebrated Israel's seventy-third year as a sovereign nation. This country is my home. Home is not where I shelter or sleep or love, but a place that can recognize me as its own. Home is where strangers are family, where emotional and biological material are unbounded by thousands of years of co-existence.

I arrived in time to observe Israel's sixty-fourth anniversary. Now, nine years have passed and I am no longer an observer. Hundreds of people of every age, size, hair, eye, and skin color mill about at the edges of the beach, waiting eagerly for the IDF, the Israel Defense Force, air show to begin the Independence Day celebration. As I lean my bicycle against a palm tree between the beach and the promenade, I move as one of them, naturally among the celebrants dancing to traditional Hebrew folk songs. With their arms raised up high, the dancers sway to the music and seem to be part of an oscillating system, everyone knowing their place.

What lay on my chromosomes may have preordained that should I find myself in this place, surrounded by people to whom my connection runs thousands of years deep, I would know I was home, and that I am no longer an outsider because of how I am built. Here, the networks of my brain that have so meticulously organized themselves around the language of survival have become a bit less fearful, though I am no less aware of my place in a world that has tried time and again to eliminate me, my ancestors, and my progeny from humankind.

Around me I hear random utterances in a language made fluent by centuries of struggle for existence.

"Aren't they beautiful?" asks a voice softly.

The woman speaking to me is looking at the dancers. She is young, perhaps no more than twenty. Her eyes are blue, and the heavy dark hair on her shoulders is pinned with a barrette at the side. A small girl holds her hand, tugging on it restlessly.

"Let's go, let's go!" The child's high voice conveys urgency as she bounces on her heels.

"Soon," the woman tells her. "The planes are coming in a few minutes. It's not time yet."

"Then let's go play on the sand until they come!" she insists.

"Yes," the woman says, "that's a good idea." Smiling, she allows herself to be pulled away by the little girl. I want to say something to her. I feel an impulse to reach out to touch her, to know she is real, and to assure her by assuring myself that we are home, and safe. But the child has already begun to lead the young woman onto the sand. Their figures merge into the shoreline as they move closer to the sea. As their images blur in the bright sunlight, their voices still penetrate the noise of the wind and the waves. The last words I can make out are:

"We need to go! It's…_____ time!"

"Come, _____Chava!"

Chava.

To the west across the sea lay Auschwitz-Birkenau, now a museum exhibiting its obscene ruined machinery of genocide. Between me and that distant relic stands my mother's Aunt Chava and her baby boy Anshel. Hers was a voice I would not hear, but I could feel her in the air around me. Had I possessed one more sense, could I have touched them? Or was this my genetic memory at work again, showing me a picture as clear as day as they made their journey from the darkness of Birkenau to a light so bright that once in it, you can never be quite sure if what you are seeing is in the distance or in your heart. I spoke to Chava from my heart.

"Can you see it, Chava? This is all yours. It all came from you and your child. You and Anshel and the little girl you comforted in her final moments were lost to us, but this country is yours, your home forever. They created it for you."

Then the planes came. Their engines drowned out the sound of the wind and the waves, and their silver bodies pushed the sunlight back to the sky as they announced with a thunderous roar, "Never again, Chava. Never again."

FOOTNOTES

Chapter 2

1. Centers for Disease Control and Prevention, Genomics and Precision Health. *What is epigenetics?* Retrieved August 29, 2022, from https: //www.cdc.gov/genomics/disease/epigenetics.htm

2. Dr. Natan Kellerman. (2013, September) Epigenetic transmission of Holocaust trauma: Can nightmares be inherited? *The Israel Journal of Psychiatry and Related Sciences.*

ACKNOWLEDGMENTS

This book started with a dream I had seven years ago. In it, my older son was smiling at me and his face was full of love. Since then, this journey has brought me much-needed understanding of my children and subsequently a great deal of healing.

I believe that the writing of this book might have remained just a deeply felt longing without the help of my dearest friends who read its every incarnation: from amorphous and disjointed memories of events that were frozen in my mind like paintings, to a structured manuscript with chapters, to the final edited work. They include my mother and inspiration, Lucy Lipiner, a Holocaust Survivor and author who now, at the age of eighty-nine, devotes herself to de-bunking Holocaust deniers; Lisa Davis, my darling sidekick since college who refused to let me hide from life; and Nancy Krulik, fearless pal for over two decades, who with her love and gentle honesty helped me climb out of the rabbit's hole on occasions too numerous to count. These three women held me up through the worst of it. I am grateful to Daphne Algom, my first and most perceptive friend in Tel-Aviv, who reminded me to make this story my own, and to the delightful Michelle King, who with her intensely thoughtful feedback, revealed the soul of a literature professor. To Chetan Mahajan, thank you for your guidance, insight, and support.

To my editors: Sandra Wendel, whose enthusiasm, support, and belief in my story helped bring the first draft alive, and to Janet Tilden, whose quiet interventions never strove to influence my sometimes odd style, but who worked instead to elicit deeper truths. To Lisa Pelto, who kept me grounded with her professionalism and kindness in bringing my book to life. And thank you, Ellie Godwin, for your clear and forward-looking thoughts.

To Dr. Rhonda Adessky, who belongs to that magnificent and rare breed of psychologist who lives to help others find peace. To Hen Mazzig, whose quest to understand the personal and societal impact of his origins helped me to understand mine. And to the wonderful readers of my early draft, thank you from the bottom of my heart. Your comments and care were invaluable to me. This group includes Jackie Batston, Vicky DeCoster, Marjorie Ehlers, Bonnie Feldstein, Darla Glazorina, Peggy Kappy, Judy Kass, Warren Marcus, Merrylue Martin, Kaylene Powell Sasse, Barbara Orzechowski, Joe Scheideler, Mary Anne Shepard, Darya Silman, Lorrie Tishler, Barbara Vannoy, and Terry Wheeler. To Anaïs and Chloe, for their support over the last twenty years; thank you for always holding tight and not letting go.

To my husband, Ron Katz, I am sure that any reader of this book knows who you are to me, but maybe they have also learned the man you are.

Finally, to my precious boys, I love you with every cell of my being.

ABOUT THE AUTHOR

Rena Lipiner Katz was born in New York and raised by parents whose lives were irrevocably shaped by the trauma of the Holocaust. She is a mother who has struggled to raise her children to be undefined by this trauma but has found it to be an elusive goal. Rena is a writer and entrepreneur who lives in Tel-Aviv with her husband Ron and their intrepid Italian sheepdog Wilbur.

4/23

Made in United States
North Haven, CT
16 October 2022